LET'S GO
ANTHROPOLOGY
Travels
on the
Internet

LET'S GO
ANTHROPOLOGY
Travels
on the
Internet

Joan Ferrante
Northern Kentucky University

Wadsworth Publishing Company
I(T)P® An International Thomson Publishing Company

Belmont, CA • Albany, NY • Bonn • Boston • Cincinnati
Detroit • Johannesburg • London • Madrid • Melbourne • Mexico City
New York • Paris • Singapore • Tokyo • Toronto • Washington

Printed in the United States of America
1 2 3 4 5 6 7 8 9 10

For more information, contact Wadsworth Publishing Company,
10 Davis Drive, Belmont, CA 94002, or electronically at
http://www.thomson.com/wadsworth.html

International Thomson
Publishing Europe
Berkshire House 168-173
High Holborn
London, WC1V 7AA, England

International Thomson
Publishing GmbH
Königswinterer Strasse 418
53227 Bonn, Germany

Thomas Nelson Australia
102 Dodds Street
South Melbourne 3205
Victoria, Australia

International Thomson
Publishing Asia
221 Henderson Rd.
#05-10 Henderson Building
Singapore 0315

Nelson Canada
1120 Birchmount Road
Scarborough, Ontario
Canada M1K 5G4

International Thomson
Publishing Japan
Hirakawacho Kyowa bldg, 3F
2-2-1 Hirakawacho
Chiyoda-ku, Tokyo 102, Japan

International Thomson
Publishing Southern Africa
Building 18, Constantia Park
240 Old Pretoria Road
Halfway House, 1685 South Africa

International Thomson
Editores
Campos Eliseos 385, Piso 7
Col Polanco
11560 México D.F. México

ISBN 0-534-53113-X

Table of Contents

Preface

Let's Go Anthropology was created with the help of six students enrolled in an applied research course. On the first day of class, when I announced that we would make *Let's Go Anthropology* a class project, only two students seemed comfortable with the plan. Several students dropped the class and others who had never been on the Internet were visibly uncomfortable with the idea but were "stuck" with the class because it was a requirement. These students viewed the Internet (and even the computer) as something mysterious and beyond their comprehension.

Over the course of a few weeks it became clear to them that, while the technology could be mastered quite easily, the most challenging task was sifting through, organizing, comprehending, and evaluating the staggering and ever-increasing amount of information people from around the world have posted on the Internet, most of which has not been evaluated in a formal way for accuracy or worth. This challenge can be traced to the fact that on the one hand, the Internet has the power to put the most meaningful, thought-provoking, and influential information available at one's fingertips. On the other hand, the Internet also gives easy and equal access to superficial, inaccurate, and sometimes offensive material. As one indicator of the massive amount of information on the Internet consider that the keywords "anthropology," "archaeology," and "linguistics" generated 19,067, 12,624 and 159,300 references, respectively. These facts point to the challenge we faced in creating *Let's Go Anthropology*: plugging in anthropology-related keywords and then sifting and sorting through thousands of documents to find high-quality Web sites students find useful in anthropology courses.

The student contributors are primarily applied cultural studies majors/minors. The applied program integrates the disciplines of sociology and anthropology and strives to prepare its majors for a career in an information-based global society by giving them a strong background in research methods and cultural diversity. An appreciation for cultural diversity within and between groups ensures that in gathering information, students venture outside the familiar and comfortable confines of their own social circles for input and feedback.

Student Contributors

Julie Anthe transferred to Northern Kentucky University from University of Massachusetts in 1995. She is a sociology major with a minor in women's studies. Julie has played the piano for 15 years and was recently promoted to assistant manager of the bank at which she works.

Jenny DeCant is a sociology major and criminology minor. Jenny transferred to NKU in spring 1996 from the University of Cincinnati. She plans to graduate before the new millennium. She is particularly interested in elite deviance and sociology of the environment.

Phyllis Miles is an applied cultural studies major with minors in Native American studies and journalism. In spring 1996 she did ethnographic research at a nursing home (*Caring for the Aged—A Stigma in American Society*). Phyllis is in the process of creating a directory of Internet resources related to North American Indians.

Renee Riegler graduated in May 1997 with an English major and an applied cultural studies minor. She is also a member of the English honors society. In spring 1997 Renee did ethnographic research on a community devastated by floods (*Floating Fieldwork: An Ethnography of a Flooded Community*). While at NKU she was editor of the spring issue of *Cameo* (creative writing and short stories, poems and prose of NKU students). She served as assistant for the national journal *Licking River Review* (300-350 annual submissions) and for *Pentangle* (a journal of the English honorary society, Sigma Tau Delta).

Grant Smith is an anthropology and an applied cultural studies major. He is particularly interested in statistical analysis and ethnographic research. Grant is doing research on "Real TV" and the messages it sends to viewers about what constitutes personal success or failure. When he is not in school, Grant works in computer sales.

Kristie Vise is an applied cultural studies major and a sociology minor with an area of concentration in women's studies. She was awarded a Dean's Scholarship for the 1997-98 academic year. Kristie is a member of the Golden Key Honor Society, Phi Theta Kappa Honor Society, and Alpha Kappa Delta Sociology Honor Society. In spring 1997, Kristie did ethnographic research at a preschool (*Everything I Need to Know I Learned in Preschool: An Ethnographic Study of Learning in a Preschool*). Kristie works as a tutor on campus and is a statistics tutor. Even though *Let's Go Anthropology* was not yet complete at semester's end, Kristie continued to work on it for an additional two months, seeing the book to completion. She is currently working on an Internet resource guide titled *Social Issues on the Internet*.

As part of the class project student contributors also interviewed anthropology professors and students to obtain constructive feedback on the structure of and topics covered in *Let's Go Anthropology*. We offer our deepest thanks to the following people for their thoughtful suggestions:

Dr. James F. Hopgood
Dr. MaryCarol Hopkins
Dr. Andrew Kipnis
Dr. Sharlotte Neely
Dr. Barbara Thiel
Ms. Dana Hildebrand
Ms. Ann Kleemeier

We also thank Dr. Frank Stallings, professor emeritus of Literature and Language at Northern Kentucky University , for reading and commenting on this manuscript. Finally we thank Dean Rogers Redding (College of Arts and Science, NKU) and Dr. Jim Hopgood (Chair, Department of Sociology, Anthropology, and Philosophy) for supporting this project with several laptop computers that students could check out for home use.

An Introduction to the Internet

Tim Berners-Lee, at the World Wide Web Consortium Lab for Computer Science at MIT, predicts that in the next several years, the Internet will contain virtually everything that has ever been written, produced, filmed, photographed, recorded, painted, or otherwise created. The paradox is that, on the one hand, the Internet has the power to put the most meaningful, thought provoking, and/or influential information available at one's fingertips. At the same time the Internet also gives easy access to inaccurate, superficial, inconsequential and sometimes offensive material.

In *Overload and Boredom: Essays on the Quality of Life in an Information Society,* Orrin Klapp offers a vivid metaphor that applies to the problem of sorting through and keeping up with the massive amounts of information that can be accessed via the Internet. Klapp envisioned a person "seated at a table fitting [together] pieces of a gigantic jigsaw puzzle. From a funnel overhead, pieces are pouring onto the table faster than one can fit them together. Most of the pieces do not match up. Indeed they do not belong to the same puzzle" (Klapp 1986, p. 110). The pieces falling from overhead represent research accumulating at a pace that interferes with people's ability to organize it into comprehensible patterns.

The idea for *Let's Go Anthropology* evolved as a reaction to the problem of information overload. This book directs readers to some of the most anthropologically useful information posted on the Internet. *Let's Go Anthropology* is not a book about the Internet. There are already many books about the Internet on the market for those who wish to learn its extensive vocabulary and to acquire skills that go beyond those needed for this book. Consequently this introduction covers only what you need to know to access Internet sites included in this book. Specifically you need to know the answers to the following questions: 1. What is the Internet? 2. What is the World Wide Web? 4. What is a browser? 5. What is a URL? 6. What is a search engine? 7. What is a local Internet provider?

What is the Internet?

The Internet is a vast network of computer networks. A computer network is a system of computers connected to one another via special software and phone, fiber optics, or other types of lines. The Internet connects tens of thousands of in-house computer networks maintained by businesses, libraries, government agencies, universities, and private organizations.

What is the World Wide Web?

The World Wide Web (WWW) is one of several Internet-based services (others include e-mail and Usenet, a discussion/newsgroup service.) The Web is a constantly changing and an ever-expanding information-sharing tool, which facilitates the exchange of text-, video-, and audio-based information. Because no one owns the Web or manages its content, it is impossible to estimate the number of computer networks that are part of the Web or to estimate the amount of information available for exchange. According to one estimate there are 500,000 (and counting) documents available through the Web (Steinberg 1996). The Web's most valuable quality is that most of the documents available for access are formatted according to standard specification known as HTML (hypertext markup language). Hypertext connects documents to one another and allows readers to move quickly via links within and across documents located anywhere on the WWW. Links are highlighted words or images that set them apart from the rest of a document's text. After readers choose a link, or click a link with a mouse, they move elsewhere. Any browser can read any basic HTML document unless the HTML format has special features that can be read only by particular browsers.

What Is a Browser?

Users access information on the Web with a browser. There are two kinds of browsers: character-based client browsers and graphical client browsers. Character-based browsers read only letters, numbers, spaces and nongraphical marks or signs and users use arrow keys and the space bar to navigate through documents. The most popular character browser is Lynx. Graphical browsers can process characters, images, and sounds. Two popular graphical browsers are Netscape Navigator and Microsoft Internet Explorer.

What is a URL?

Every document on the Internet has an address called a Uniform Resource Locator. Some examples of Uniform Resource Locators are
(1) http://www.usatoday.com/news/nweird.htm
(2) http://library.whitehouse.gov/PressReleases-plain.cgi
(3) gopher://wings.buffalo.edu/11/academic/department/anthropology/ jwa
(4) ftp://vela.acs.oakland.edu/pub/anthap/Problems_with_ anthropologists_use_of_libraries
(5) http://www.wri.org
(6) http://www.worldculture.com/

Though rules for URLs are very loose, they contain a basic structure. Ninety percent of the WWW URLs listed in Sociology on the Internet begin with http://; 9.9% of the URLs begin with gopher:// and a very few begin with ftp://. "http" stands for hypertext transfer protocol. "ftp" stands for file transfer protocol. Protocol is a system of procedures to access information. "gopher" is the mascot of the University of Minnesota, home of the Internet navigational tool that facilitates the search for information.

The **domain name system** or the host computer name lies between the double slashes (//) and the first single slash mark (/). It is called a domain name system because it makes reference to several domains or areas within an in-house computer network. Each domain is separated by a period. Notice that most domain name systems listed in the six examples above end with a three letter code: .org, .com, .gov, or .edu. This tells us that the host computer is an organization (.org), a company (.com), a government agency (.gov), or an educational institution (.edu). Sometimes the domain name system ends with a two-letter code .uk (or .us, or .tr) known as county codes. For example, .uk stands for United Kingdom.

To the left of these two-digit or three-digit codes are usually some clues about the identity of the organization, company, government agency, or educational institution. It's easy to see that the first URL refers to the company USAToday and the second URL is the White House, a department within the U.S. government. In the third example "buffalo" stands for Buffalo University, and in the fourth "oakland" stands for Oakland University. In the fifth example, "wri" stands for World Resources Institute. The last URL refers to the company World Culture.

The information between the single slashes is code for the directories or hypertext paths one must follow to get to a particular document. Clues about the name or kind of document to which the URL takes you are to the far right of the URL address. If there are no paths, as in examples 5 and 6, the URL takes you to the host institutions' opening pages or home pages. The documents for each of the six examples follow:

Document

(1) nweird.htm	weird news stories
(2) Press Releases-plian.cgi	press releases
(3) jwa	Journal of World Anthropology
(4) Problems_with_anthropologists_ use_of_libraries	Problems with anthropologists use of libraries
(5) No paths specified in URL	
(6) No paths specified in URL	

To gain access to these documents you simply type in the URL at the appropriate place designated by the browser. In the case of the Lynx browser, simply type the letter 'g' and begin typing the URL in the designated space. In the case of Netscape Navigator, delete the URL appearing in the location box and type the URL you wish to locate in its place.

How do you find URLs? URL addresses can be found in many different places. Like this book, there are URL "Yellow Pages" that are organized by subject with relevant URL addresses. Sometimes corporations and agencies will list their URL addresses in an advertisement. For example, at the end of the Lehrer Newshour, PBS lists its URL, which is http://www.pbs.org. Another way to find URLs is via search engines.

What Is a Search Engine?
A search engine allows users to submit a keyword or words to identify the topic for which they wish to find information. The search engine identifies Web sites and corresponding URLs that lead to information on that topic. Some names of search engines are InfoSeek, Yahoo, CUSI, Starting Point, Lycos, Webcrawler, and Excite. Because there is so much information on the Web and no central authority managing its contents, "organizing the Web is probably the hardest information science problem out there" (Yang in Steinberg 1996, p. 109). Search engines try "to bring order out of chaos in a frantic quest for the ultimate index of human knowledge" (Steinberg 1996, p. 109). Yahoo indexers, for example, claim to have catalogued more than 200,000 Web sites (and counting) into 20,000 different categories (Steinberg 1996). To gain access to a search engine and browser (and by extension, the Internet) you need to find a local Internet access provider.

What is a Local Internet Access Provider?

Most people can not afford their own direct connection to the Internet. Consequently they rely on a **local Internet access provider**, a nearby host institution which offers Internet access via a local telephone call as a benefit of membership or for a fee. Many students can get access to the Internet through their school or university. Some businesses and other organizations offer their employees or members access. Public libraries give access to patrons. Then there are dozens of commercial Internet service providers who offer the connection for a fee (ranging from $10 dollars a month and up depending on use). Examples include American Online, Prodigy, Compuserve, and perhaps your local telephone company.

To access the portion of the Internet known as the World Wide Web from home you must have a personal computer, a modem, and modem software (don't panic) which allows you to connect to a provider's host computer via dial-up telephone line. You will have to find out from your local Internet service provider about software and other details in order to connect to their service from your home.

If you are a student and do not have a personal computer and/or the necessary equipment to connect to the Internet from your home, check out the availability of public computer labs located in dorms, academic departments, libraries and other places on campus.

Some Words of Advice

We close with some advice from Internet experts. The students who worked on this and other Internet projects have learned from experience how to handle the Internet. Their suggestions can save you a lot of headaches. You might want to try some Internet sites before you read the advice.

The first few times I used the Internet I felt like a lost traveler in a foreign land. I visited many sites but either came up empty-handed or overwhelmed. An information society gives us the opportunity to access thousands of documents but the sheer volume can leave us unable to recall what we have read. So my advice is to search the Internet with a goal in mind and keep focused on that goal. **Renee Riegler**

I learned about the Internet and computers at the same time. In the beginning there were several times I was so frustrated that I just walked away from the computer so discouraged that I thought I would have to drop the class (if only it were not required). I found that the best way to deal with that frustration was to go to the computer lab and ask questions of other students working around me. **Jenny DeCant**

My advice to someone using the Internet for the first time, or even thinking about it, is to just do it! Don't be afraid of the technology. For so long I felt like everyone else was far ahead of me in their knowledge of and experience with computers. There were times (and there still are times) I thought my 14-year old nephew would run me over on the information highway. But the only way to address fears and insecurities is to keep in mind that it is never too late to learn. **Julie Anthe**

Some of the greatest minds in history have claimed that they gained knowledge from simply reading books that were readily available at their fingertips such as dictionaries and encyclopedias. Well right at our fingertips we have access to generations of knowledge and wisdom. As I have also recommended to my own children, during your leisure time take a few minutes to plug into a search engine an unfamiliar word or phrase that you would like to know more about. You will be amazed at how much you will learn. **Phyllis Miles**

I was excited at the opportunity to learn about the Internet when I entered this class. Nearly halfway through the semester doing "search" after "search" I began to see many of the same Web sites over and over again. This was very frustrating. I had lost touch with the notion of getting on the Internet for enjoyment. Take the time to just browse the Internet for your own enjoyment. **Grant Smith**

My advice to those of you just beginning to explore the capabilities of the Internet is to keep in mind that the Internet is an invaluable "brainstorming" tool that can help identify creative topics for research papers and class projects. This is because the Internet links information together that you may never have thought of as being connected. It will also help you to come up with topics that you might never have thought of on your own. For example, imagine that you are trying to come up for a research topic for a paper for a physical anthropology class. The "Annual Editions: Physical Anthropology" Web site offers a variety of abstracts for papers relating to physical anthropology including one that applies the "Darwinian perspective" to the understanding of the evolution, mutation and natural selection of the AIDS virus. **Kristie Vise**

The Internet presents a whole new way of thinking about information. My advice is to expect change and learn to be comfortable with it. People who post information on the Internet can choose to take it off or revise it whenever they see fit. With books, authors might want to change their ideas but have to wait until the next edition (if there is a next edition) to get it out there for the world to see. With the Internet, authors can revise their thinking whenever they see fit and make changes on the spot. So don't be surprised it you find a document has changed in subtle or dramatic ways from one visit to the next. **Jenny DeBerry**

My advice is not to wait until the last minute to do Internet assignments. The Internet might not be available an hour before your assignment is due. I read an article in the *New York Times* that says it all: "More than a million computer users suffered interrupted or erratic Internet and online service connections last week because of a variety of planned and unplanned service shutdowns" (Lewis 1996, p. C1). Sometimes the "system crashes" lasted as long as eight hours. **Patricia Gaines**

My tip is to always double check the URL you typed in against the one listed in the text. It must be typed *exactly* as listed in the text. For example, lower case letters cannot be substituted for capital letters. This will prevent or solve many of the problems you might have in locating a site that you know is there but the computer is telling you isn't. Also when using a search engine such as the Web Crawler, Excite, Lycos, etc., try to think of more than one key phrase or search word. I usually try to think of eight different key words/phrases for each of my topics I am researching. Be patient and explore. You may not always find what you are looking for right away. Don't be afraid to follow hypertext links; sometimes the best information is found in the most unusual places. **Ryan Huber**

The Internet requires a person to have a great deal of patience, a low frustration level and a detective-like mentality. To get the best results for a search on the Internet, be as specific as possible with your choice of words and phrases. The Internet has so many sites that if your search word is too vague or general the search engine may generate tens of thousands of sites. I found that the hypertext words or suggested links within documents are often more valuable to my research than the document the search engine generated as directly related. Sometimes the highlighted words or links appear to have no relationship with my chosen topic. **Laureen Norris**

Sometimes the Internet can be very slow. You have to wait 20 or 30 seconds (imagine that!) for the document to appear after you type in the URL. My advice is to try nonpeak-hour times before 9:00 a.m. and after 5:00 p.m. The fewer the people on the Internet, the faster the response time. **Julie Rack**

The amount of information on the WWW is massive. You can find something on almost any topic. However, you must be mentally and physically tough when searching for information on the Web. Sometimes you can feel totally overwhelmed to the point of panic. But don't worry, most people feel this way at one time or another. My advice is to relax and to not feel that you have to look or read over everything on a topic. **Jacob Stewart**

Be patient with the Internet, but don't spend too much time at any one site. Remember the Internet has information on every subject; it's just a matter of finding it. Look through sites quickly, and if the information doesn't seem useful to the task at hand, keep going and don't look back. Above all, take an "I'm in charge" attitude. Don't let the Internet overwhelm you. Maneuvering around the Internet is an acquired skill. The more time you spend at it, the more efficient you'll become. **Angela Vaughn**

I could list a hundred little tips about the Internet, but I will offer just one. Many Web sites are rearranged or restructured on a regular basis so that the path one takes to get to a document might change. When that happens, a URL address listed in the textbook may not get you to the document. Don't be alarmed if you type in a URL and the message "unable to connect to remote host" or "a path does not exit" appears. The chances are very good that the document is still there but that the "path" has changed. So what do you do? You could take the easy way out and tell the instructor, "The URL doesn't work; I can't do the assignment," or with a little effort you could try to find the document yourself. Here's what you do. Type in the entire URL. Begin by erasing the address back to the first slash. So if your URL is **http://www.lawrence.edu/~peregrip/seahome.html,** then erase **/seahome.html** and submit the revised address. If that revised address doesn't work, erase the address back to the next slash. In the case of the example above, you will erase **/~peregrip**. Keep doing this until you have only the domain name system to submit. If you gain access, search for hypertext links that match up with path code names in your original URL. Hopefully this will not happen too often, but if it does, you know what to do. Good luck. **Lindsay Hixson**

Tips on Using *Let's Go Anthropology: Travels on the Internet*

There are many URL directories, known as "Internet yellow pages" on the market, some 600 to 700 pages long. Virtually all these directories try to be everything to everybody by including URLs related to almost every conceivable topic and interest (herbs, sports, online dating, jokes, gardening, games, home maintenance, skateboarding, oceanography, pornography, poetry, philosophy, and science fiction). In addition to offering a smorgasbord of information sources, the accompanying descriptions are often too general to help users evaluate the quality and kind of information posted on a site without going there first.

Let's Go Anthropology: Travels on the Internet is a URL directory created with the anthropology student in mind. It includes a list of URLs that take you to Web sites containing information that can help you do many college assignments, but especially those related to anthropology, without leaving your desk. (This will save wear and tear on you, your car, and the environment). It is estimated that there are over 250 URL addresses in this book that will lead you to sites offering a wide range of information from "accepted abbreviations for international organizations and groups" to "zip-code-level data."

Although we have also tried to select Web sites that contain high-quality information and to write concise descriptions that specify the kinds of information you will find there, we suggest that, to get the most of this URL directory, you spend an hour or so reading and/or skimming the entries in the book. First, this will help you to appreciate the extraordinary capacity of the Internet to put a wide range of high quality information at your fingertips. Second, once you grasp the range of resources named in this book, you will be in a better position to respond to a variety of assignments (essays, term papers, research studies, posters, presentations, maps, and so on) in creative, flexible, and efficient ways. Your response can be creative because you have a range of thought-provoking and interesting resources from which to choose. You can be flexible because you can explore your resource options quickly. Finally, you can be efficient because you can spend the time on your assignment that you would have spent driving to and from the library, tracking down sources, and standing in line to photocopy needed materials.

In addition we have a number of specific suggestions that will help in your search for the information you need:
• One of the hazards of the Internet is that URL addresses can

9

change or even disappear forever. When a URL does not work, several things could be wrong: the server is down, Internet use is very high, the URL has changed, or the document has been removed temporarily or even permanently. To address this challenge my advice is to follow Lindsay Hixson's advice on page 11 or to simply plug the document name into one of the search engines. Ninety-five percent of the time the latter method will yield results.

• For the most part there are no separate entries for individual countries or cultures. If you are looking for information on a specific country, we suggest that you go to the country-level section of this directory. Pay special attention to "Country Background Notes" and the "World Factbook," both of which contain information on every country in the world.

• If you are in the early stages of an assignment and you are simply looking for an interesting idea or an unusual angle on a well-known topic check out "Anthropology in the News" and the "Online News Hour."

• If you would like to explore some Web sites in order to become acquainted with the Internet we recommend the following five URLs:

   • "Cultural Exchange" at:
      http://www.deil.lang.uiuc.edu/exchange/
   • "Emoticons" at:
      http://www.organic.com/1800collect/Emoticons/index.html
   • "Movie Database" at:
      http://us.imdb.com/tour.html
   • "Encyclopedia of the Orient" at:
      http://i-cias.com/e.o/index.htm
   • "Documents in the News" at:
      http://www.lib.umich.edu/libhome/Documents.center/
      docnews.html

• Finally, be a responsible "netizen," or citizen of the Internet. Read "Declarations of the Rights [and Responsibilities] of Netizens" at http://www.columbia.edu/~rh120/. Take time to e-mail people and organizations to thank them (or their sponsors) if you find useful the information they have posted.

Part I

Anthropology Resources on the Internet

Africa—South of the Sahara

Africa
http://sunsite.berkeley.edu/

The Librarians' Index to the Internet includes the category "Africa." Select that category and find links to Web sites such as "African News," "Africa Online," and "Contemporary Conflicts in Africa."

African Art Gallery
http://www.afrinet.net/gallery

This site is maintained by AfriNET Gallery whose mission is to provide "the finest and most comprehensive collection of African American, Caribbean and African Art available today." This site includes "original art, graphics (traditional printmaking techniques such as serigraphy, lithography and etching), fine art prints, posters, sculptures, and mixed media." This site is best viewed using Netscape.

Africa News on the World Wide Web
http://www.africanews.org/aboutano.html

African News Online is part of the Africa News Service, a non-profit U.S. news agency founded in 1973. "African News Service has been directly or indirectly responsible for a significant percentage of U.S. media coverage of Africa, generating public and policy attention to the least-covered continent." The news service publishes current stories from the African press and from the Pan-Africa News Agency (the largest news gathering operation in Africa) as well as special reports and publications.

African Art: Aesthetics and Meaning
http://www.lib.virginia.edu/dic/exhib/93.ray.aa/African.html

This site contains "a catalog of an exhibition of African art at the Bayly Museum, University of Virginia." The purpose of this exhibit is to examine the "formal aesthetic aspects of the objects and the moral and religious ideas they express." This site includes an introductory guide explaining the meaning and "elements of African aesthetics," as well as an online exhibition of African art. For each exhibit, there is a brief description focusing on the aesthetic value and meaning of the piece and on the materials used to create the piece. Included in the description is information on the region of Africa from which the artwork originated. Must be viewed using Netscape.

African Links on the Internet
http://www.yale.edu/swahili/afrilink.html

This site posts an extensive list of Internet links related to Africa and specific African countries including environmental news, weather information, travel guides and information, maps, factbooks, music, and art.

African Studies WWW (U. Penn)
http://www.sas.upenn.edu/African_Studies/AS.html

The African Studies Center at the University of Pennsylvania has created a virtual library of resources for each African country. Choose Algeria, for example, and you have access to a map of the country, the U.S. State Department Travel Advisory on that country, the Algerian embassy in the U.S., and the *World Factbook* entry for Algeria as well as a variety of other online resources including news, personal home pages of Algerian scholars working around the world, a list of schools in Algeria, and much more.

Karen Fung's African Links
http://www-sul.stanford.edu/depts/ssrg/africa/guide.html

Karen Fung, Deputy Curator, Africa Collection, Hoover Library at Stanford University, has prepared a list of selected Internet resources for the Electronic Technology Group, African Studies Association. The Internet resources are organized by topic and region. There are links to topics from A ("African Studies Programs") to W ("Women"). This is an excellent resource guide.

Nok—The Museum of African Art @Harlemm
http://harlemm.com/nokbeta/

The Nok Museum of African Arts is a virtual museum "dedicated to the study, preservation and exhibition of all forms of African art and its derivatives." The museum maintains "an electronic collection of works held by other museums and private collectors." This site is best viewed using Netscape.

Anthro-Futurism

AnthroFuturism
http://www.clas.ufl.edu/users/seeker1/cyberanthro/AnthroFuturis
m.html

Traditionally, the discipline of anthropology has focused on past cultures out of a concern that technology and modernization was causing them to disappear. This essay examines a new form of anthropology, AnthroFuturism, which uses the anthropological perspective to predict and describe changes taking place in society in light of technological "advances." "While "futurists" have speculated on the inevitability of change and the opportunities change brings, AnthroFuturists do not see change as necessarily inevitable, unavoidable, or desirable." AnthroFuturists speculate on "what if" scenarios. For example, how might culture change *if* extraterrestrial life forms exist, *if* life expectancy is extended significantly, or in light of genetic engineering.

Anthropological Societies and Organizations

American Academy of Forensic Sciences
http://www.aafs.org/

The American Academy for Forensic Science draws members from a wide range of professions: "physicians, criminologists, toxicologists, attorneys, dentists, physical anthropologists, document examiners, engineers, psychiatrists, educators, and others who practice and perform research in the many diverse fields relating to forensic science." Membership is open to pre-professionals (students) and professionals. The academy posts only the most basic information related to its membership and annual meeting.

American Anthropological Association
http://www.ameranthassn.org/

The American Anthropological Association, founded in 1902, aims "to promote the science of anthropology, to stimulate and coordinate the efforts of American anthropologists, to foster local and other societies devoted to anthropology, to serve as a bond among American anthropologists and anthropologic(al) organizations present and prospective, and to publish and encourage the publication of matter

14

pertaining to anthropology." This site contains a wealth of information. Of particular interest are a survey of anthropology Ph.D.s and an overview of career opportunities in anthropology. The AAA posts information on 32 subsections/associations and on its 24 publications. A search engine is available to use keywords such as "archaeology" or "linguistics" to conduct a search for relevant documents.

The following is a listing of the subsections/associations and their URL endings, which may be directly accessed at:
http://www.ameranthassn.org/

American Ethnological Society	**aes.htm**
Anthropology and Environment Section	**ae.htm**
Archaeology Division	**ad.htm**
Association for Africanist Anthropology	**afaa.htm**
Association of Black Anthropologists	**aba.htm**
Association for Feminist Anthropology	**afa.htm**
Association of Latina and Latino Anthropologists	**alla.htm**
Association for Political and Legal Anthropology	**apla.htm**
Association of Senior Anthropologists	**asa.htm**
Biological Anthropology Section	**bas.htm**
Central States Anthropological Society	**csas.htm**
Council on Anthropology and Education	**cae.htm**
Council for General Anthropology	**cga.htm**
Council for Museum Anthropology	**cma.htm**
Council on Nutritional Anthropology	**can.htm**
Culture and Agriculture	**cag.htm**
Middle East Section	**mes.htm**
National Association for the Practice of Anthropology	**apa.htm**
National Association of Student Anthropologists	**asa.htm**
Society for Anthropology in Community Colleges	**sacc.htm**
Society for the Anthropology of Consciousness	**sac.htm**
Society for the Anthropology of Europe	**sae.htm**
Society for the Anthropology of North America	**sana.htm**
Society for the Anthropology of Work	**saw.htm**
Society for Cultural Anthropology	**sca.htm**
Society for Humanistic Anthropology	**sha.htm**
Society for Latin American Anthropology	**slaa.htm**
Society for Linguistic Anthropology	**sla.htm**
Society for Medical Anthropology	**sma.htm**
Society for Psychological Anthropology	**spa.htm**
Society for Urban Anthropology	**sua.htm**
Society for Visual Anthropology	**sva.htm**

American Folklore Society
http://gopher.panam.edu:70/1gopher_root10%3a%5b000000%5d

The *American Folklore Society Newsletter* publishes interesting articles and information. Unfortunately the newsletters are long, and there is no table of contents, so you have to browse each one to see what they contain. However, if you have to do general research on folklore, the time it takes to browse the newsletters will pay off with useful results.

American Oriental Society
http://www-personal.umich.edu/~jrodgers/

The American Oriental Society, maintained by the University of Michigan, encourages "basic research in the languages and literature of Asia." The table of contents for the most recent *Journal of the American Oriental Society* and for the society's newsletter is available. The newsletter can be downloaded. The most useful information for students is the Proposed Guidelines for Professional Ethics for the American Oriental Society.

Canadian Association of Palynologists
http://gpu.srv.ualberta.ca/~abeaudoi/cap/cap.html

The Canadian Association of Palynologists (CAP) was founded in 1978. The objective of the Society is to "advance and encourage all aspects of palynology in Canada and to promote co-operation between palynologists and those engaged in related fields of study." This site offers selected publications from the CAP newsletter, including articles such as "Palynology and the Mole Cricket" and "Aquilapollenites: Carved in Stone!"

Canadian Sociology and Anthropology Association
http://artsci-ccwin.concordia.ca/SocAnth/csaa/csaa_hm.html

The Canadian Sociology and Anthropology Association "promotes research, publication, and teaching in Anthropology and Sociology in Canada." The society publishes a journal, *The Canadian Review of Sociology and Anthropology*. Newsletters are published monthly and the two most recent issues are online. Of particular interest to students are the links to sociology and anthropology departments in Canada. The association also posts information on its annual conference, membership, and ethics.

Commission on Theoretical Anthropology (COTA) Web Page
http://www.univie.ac.at/voelkerkunde/theoretical-
anthropology/cota.html

The Commission on Theoretical Anthropology was formed in 1993 as
an open forum promoting the exchange of ideas among anthropologists
of various theoretical and methodological traditions. The Web site
offers access to the most recent newsletter, which was posted in 1994.
This Web site is listed, not because it has a lot of up-to-date
information, but because the idea of opening and supporting such a
forum is valuable in itself.

Dental Anthropology Association
http://www.sscf.ucsb.edu/~walker/index.html

The Dental Anthropology Association, maintained by the University of
California at Santa Barbara, seeks to "stimulate interest in the field of
dental anthropology and to promote the exchange of educational,
scientific, and scholarly knowledge in the field." Browse the
bibliography section for articles on dental-related topics published in
The American Journal of Physical Anthropology between 1975-1996.
The association also lists links to Web sites of interest to dental
anthropologists.

International Council of Museums (ICOM) Web Page
http://www.icom.org/

The International Council of Museums (ICOM), created in 1946 with
13,000 members in 145 countries, is "devoted to the promotion and
development of museums and the museum profession at an
international level." The site posts a chronology from 1946 to 1996 of
information pertaining to ICOM events and happenings. There is also
information on International Museum Day, created for museum
professionals to promote museum awareness. Check out the "Virtual
Library Museum Home pages," which functions as a directory of
museums that can be accessed via the Internet.

Linguistic Society of America
http://www.acls.org/acls/lingsa.htm

The Linguistic Society of America, founded in 1924 and with a
membership of 7,000, posts basic information about its organization
along with the program of its annual meetings. Of particular interest to
the student researching linguistics are the organization's statements and
resolutions on issues such as "Language Rights," "Ebonics," "Research

with Human Subjects," and "English Only Initiatives." The organization also posts a list of approximately 100 journals that publish articles related to linguistics. Finally, check out *The Field of Linguistics*, a series of 22 essays explaining and clarifying the field of linguistics. Examples of essays include "Language Diversity," "Language and Brain," "Slips of the Tongue," "History of Linguistics," "Sociolinguistics," and "Endangered Languages."

New Zealand Association of Social Anthropologists (NZASA)
http://www.massey.ac.nz/~NZSRDA/nzssorgs/nzasa/nzasa.htm

The New Zealand Association of Social Anthropologists was established in 1975 "to support the ethical conduct of social anthropology" as described in "Principles of Professional Responsibility and Ethical Conduct." In addition to information on membership and its annual meetings, NZASA also publishes electronic editions of its newsletter.

Palaeontological Association
http://www.nhm.ac.uk/paleonet/PalAss/PalAss.html

Founded in 1957, the Palaeontological Association promotes the study of palaeontology (i.e. the study of fossils as a way of gathering information about animals and plants). The Association gives access to published newsletters, field guides, and scholarly journals such as *Paleontology* and *Special Papers in Paleontology*. Current and back issues of journals and newsletters are available online. There is also information on annual meetings and field exhibitions.

The Royal Anthropological Institute of Great Britain and Ireland—RAI
http://lucy.ukc.ac.uk/rai/

The Royal Anthropological Institute of Great Britain and Ireland, a not-for-profit organization established in 1843, is the world's oldest ongoing anthropological organization with members from around the world. The Institute gives a broad overview of its history and the table of contents for the most recent issues of *Anthropology Today* and the *Journal of the Royal Anthropological Institute*. You can search the Anthropological Index online, which compiles entries from more than 750 journals received by the Department of Ethnography Library.

SAAweb - Society for American Archaeology
http://www.saa.org/

The Society for American Archaeology, founded in 1934, has more than 5,600 members who are "dedicated to the research, interpretation, and protection of the archaeological heritage of the Americas." At this site you can find information related to membership, publications, conferences, bylaws, and other archaeological information. Of particular interest to students are an answer to the question "What is archaeology?", an overview of career opportunities in archaeology; the document, *Principles of Archaeological Ethics*; and the *Society for American Archaeology Bulletin*. The *Bulletin* contains interesting articles, essays, and news. Examples from the November 1996 issue include "9,300-Year-Old Skeleton Sparks Controversy in Northwest," "Working Together—The Archaeological Field Schools in the 1990's," and "Student Affairs-Getting Graphics! Making an Effective Poster."

Society for Applied Anthropology
http://zoom1.telepath.com:80/sfaa/

The Society for Applied Anthropology, founded in 1941, has 2,000 members from a variety of academic and applied backgrounds in anthropology and other disciplines as well. The common bond members share is a desire to "make an impact on the quality of life in the world today." The society seeks to investigate and identify principles of human behavior and apply those principles to address contemporary issues and problems. At this site you can find information related to membership, publications, conferences, bylaws, and other applied organizations.

The Society for Economic Anthropology
http://www.lawrence.edu/~peregrip/seahome.html

The Society for Economic Anthropology is interested in "understanding diversity and change in the economic systems around the world." The society sponsors an annual student paper competition and publishes the entire text of the 1993-1996 graduate and undergraduate papers online. Two examples of titles are "In Defense of Collective Farms" and "Women of the Praia." Competition guidelines and instructions are available.

The Society for Historical Archaeology
http://www.azstarnet.com/~sha/

The Society for Historical Archaeology (SHA), formed in 1967, is "the largest scholarly group concerned with the archaeology of the modern world (1400-present)." The society is specifically concerned with "the identification, excavation, interpretation, and conservation of sites and materials on land and underwater" and supports "the conservation, preservation, and research of archaeological resources, including both land and underwater remains." This site offers contents and abstracts of current issues of the *Historical Archaeology Journal* and access to the society's newsletter. There is an excellent link for "Kids!" that explores the field of archaeology, career opportunities and rewards of choosing archaeology as a profession.

The Society for Linguistic Anthropology
http://www.ameranthassn.org/sla.htm

The Society for Linguistic Anthropology was founded in 1983 "to advance the study of language in its social and cultural contexts and to encourage communication of the results of such study." The society's bylaws, publications, and the names, addresses, and phone/fax numbers of its officers can be accessed.

Anthropology Clubs

NASA Guide to Anthropology Clubs
http://www.ameranthassn.org/nasabook.htm

This guide, published by the National Association of Student Anthropologists, a section within the AAA, offers information about how to start an anthropology club, themes for anthropology clubs, and ideas for club activities. This guide is available to both members and non-members of the AAA for a low fee (currently $1.00).

NAU Anthropology Club
http://dana.ucc.nau.edu/~anthro-p/

The Northern Arizona University (NAU) Anthropology Club posts information about upcoming Anthropology Club events, student home pages, student research, and internship programs.

SSU Anthropology Club
http://www.sonoma.edu/anthropology/AnClub.html

The Anthropology Club at Sonoma State University (SSU) maintains this Web site. From this site, read abstracts of papers presented at 1996 Graduate Symposium, browse M.A. thesis titles, and read about current anthropology student projects at SSU. The departmental newsletter, *Notes and Queries*, is particularly interesting because it contains ideas that other anthropology programs may also wish to adopt.

Anthropology in the News

Anthropology in the News
http://www.tamu.edu/anthropology/news.html

Where does the public get its images of anthropology? This site posts links to magazine and newspaper articles pertaining to subjects that the media connect with the discipline of anthropology. The sources of these articles include CNN, *USA Today*, MSNBC, *The New York Times*, *Scientific American,* and *National Geographic*, among others. Examples of anthropological topics that make the news are "Urban Folklore," "Ebonics," and reports on major archaeological finds.

The Center for Anthropology and Science Communications
http://chimera.acs.ttu.edu/~wurlr/anthro.html

The Center for Anthropology and Science Communications is a media resource for finding anthropologists and for communicating about anthropology "through the media, the Internet, and news and information services." Of particular interest is the section on "media anthropology," which gives a short history of the term, the "AAA Checklist for Easy and Effective Press," and suggestions for an "Effective Press Release" and for handling television interviews.

Public Broadcasting Service
http://www.pbs.org

This is the home page of the Public Broadcasting Service. This is an amazing resource for in-depth coverage of headline news and social and cultural issues in general. The quality of the material on this site defies simple summary. Start with the "Online Newshour" and browse its "past programs" and "essays and dialogues." Plug in keywords of interest to anthropologists such as specific country names, culture, archeology, Native Americans, language, etc.

Anthropology Student Projects on the Web

Anthropology Student Project Pages
http://www.lawrence.edu/dept/anthropology/student_projects.html

Lawrence University Anthropology Department posts anthropology student projects. Projects include "Social Ecology of the Chesapeake Bay," "Environmental Law," "Wildlife Management: Kenya and Zimbabwe" and "San of Botswana."

Northern Arizona Student Projects and Home Pages
http://dana.ucc.nau.edu/~anthro-p/projects.html

The Anthropology Club at Northern Arizona University posts several student projects and home pages at this Web site. Included are pages related to (1) agriculture in Madagascar, (2) American Indians, and (3) The Hopi Cultural Preservation Office.

Papers from the Institute of Archaeology
http://www.ucl.ac.uk/archaeology/pia/

"Papers from the Institute of Archaeology (PIA) was launched in 1990 by a group of research students at the Institute of Archaeology, University College London" with the goal of providing an "outlet for research at the graduate level." Selected back issues of this journal are available online, while others are available for purchase. Each online issue contains full text of articles, book reviews and abstracts of archaeology dissertations. Of particular interest are "The Problems and Prospects of Cultural Evolution" (Issue 1) and "Mortuary practices among the Aztecs in the light of ethnohistorical and archaeological sources" (Issue 4).

RV's Forensic Anthropology Home Page
http://www.acs.appstate.edu/~rr13810/

R.V. Rickard, an anthropology student with a passion for forensic anthropology at Appalachian State University in North Carolina, offers some advice to students who share his interests. Also included are several papers Rikard wrote for forensic anthropology classes.

Student Web Pages
http://www.rlc.dcccd.edu/MATHSCI/anth/homepage/stwbpgs.htm

This site contains Web pages created by students at Richland College in Dallas, Texas. These pages were constructed as requirements for three anthropology courses: Cultural Anthropology, Introduction to Archaeology, and American Indian Cultures. The Cultural Anthropology students were required to gather ethnographic information from an individual who was "enculturated in the United States during the 1930s, the decade of the great economic depression" and display a portion of their data on their Web page. The Archaeology students were "asked to choose any topic related to archeology and create a Web page report that includes an introduction, at least one graphic image, at least six hyperlinks with appropriate annotation, and a bibliography." American Indian Cultures students were required to "compose a page concerning some aspect of American Indians that includes an introduction, at least one graphic image, at least six hyperlinks with appropriate annotation, and a bibliography." This site is best viewed using Netscape.

Anthropology--What Is It?

For a general description of anthropology, visit any one (or all) of the four Web sites listed below. The University of Louisville offers the most comprehensive overview. For the briefest definition of the discipline, see the University of California, Berkeley posting.

California State University, Northridge, Anthropology Department
http://www.csun.edu/~hfant005/whatis.htm

Cornell University, Department of Anthropology
http://falcon.arts.cornell.edu/Anthro/

University of California, Berkeley
http://www.ls.berkeley.edu/Dept/Anth/whatis.html

University of Louisville, Anthropology
http://www.louisville.edu/groups/anthro-www/whatis.htm

Into the World of Anthropology
http://www.ed.uiuc.edu/stUdEnTs/B-Sklar/basic387.html

Annual Editions: Anthropology
http://www.dushkin.com/annualeditions/0-697-37201-4.mhtml

This site offers abstracts to 44 articles reprinted in *Annual Editions*: *Anthropology*. Simply reading the abstracts gives an excellent overview of the kinds of topics anthropologists study.

Applied Anthropology

Anthro L: Short Autobiographies
http://www.anatomy.su.oz.au:80/danny/anthropology/anthro-l/biographies/index.html

This site contains the names and biographies of twenty-one practicing anthropologists who are central to the list server Anthro-L, which is supported by the State University of New York at Buffalo. For those interested in a career in anthropology, read the biographies to see how others came to be practicing anthropologists.

Anthropologists at Work
http://www.oakland.edu/~dow/napafaq.htm

The National Association for the Practice of Anthropology answers some common questions students have about the field of applied anthropology. These questions are: (1) How great is the demand for practicing anthropologists? Are there jobs? (2) If I am interested in working as a practicing anthropologist, what academic degrees do I need? (3) Are there universities that offer training programs in practicing anthropology? (4) What courses should I take? What skills would be good to acquire while I am in college? (5) Would it be helpful to have internship experience? How do I get it? (6) How do I go about getting a job after graduating? What is the best way to sell myself as a practicing anthropologist? (7) Who employs practicing anthropologists? (8) How much do practicing anthropologists make? What about benefits? (9) Are many anthropologists self-employed? How do you make a living as a private consultant? (10) How are working conditions for practicing anthropologists? Are there special risks or difficulties? (11) Tell me about some of the other careers of practicing anthropologists. (12) Can students join the National Association for the Practice of Anthropology?

Applied Anthropology Documentation Project
http://www.acs.oakland.edu:80/~dow/sources1.htm

The Society for Applied Anthropology and four other applied
organizations sponsor the Applied Anthropology Documentation
Project, a series of applied project profiles, which highlight
"anthropology in action." This Web site contains only abstracts.
However, a review of these abstracts shows the various ways in which
anthropologists seek to address a wide range of problems and issues.

**Human Organization—Journal of the Society of Applied
Anthropology**
http://www.smu.edu/~anthrop/humanorg.html

Human Organization publishes manuscripts "dealing with all areas of
applied social science." At this site you can access titles and abstracts
of articles in current and forthcoming issues. If you have to write a
paper on applied anthropology, browse this site for ideas.

**National Association for the Practice of Anthropology Resource
List**
http://www.oakland.edu/~dow/napa/napares/napa.htm

This site gives information about how to become a member of the
National Association for the Practice of Anthropology (NAPA). The
benefits of membership include the NAPA Mentor Program which
provides student members and anthropologists-in-transition with
"career information, networking opportunities, training suggestions and
feedback which arise at work or in the field." There is also information
about how to subscribe to listservers, which act as discussion channels
for those concerned with technology, rural development, involuntary
resettlement, and applied anthropology. The documents,
"Anthropologists at Work" and "Training Guidelines for Applied
Anthropology Programs" can be accessed at this Web site.

Society for Applied Anthropology
http://zoom1.telepath.com:80/sfaa/

The Society for Applied Anthropology, founded in 1941, has 2,000
members from a variety of academic and applied backgrounds in
anthropology and other disciplines. The common bond members share
is a desire to "make an impact on the quality of life in the world today."
The society seeks to investigate and identify principles of human
behavior and apply those principles to address contemporary issues and

problems. At this site you can find information related to membership, publications, conferences, bylaws, and other applied organizations.

Archaeology

American Journal of Archaeology
http://classics.lsa.umich.edu/AJA.html

This is the Web site of the official journal of the Archaeological Institute of America (AJA). It contains titles (no abstracts) for forthcoming, most recent, and past issues of the journal.

Annual Editions: Archaeology
http://www.dushkin.com/annualeditions/0-697-37206-5.mhtml

This site offers abstracts to 45 articles reprinted in *Annual Editions*: *Archaeology*. Simply reading the abstracts gives an excellent overview of the kinds of topics archaeologists study.

Archaeological Fieldwork Opportunities
http://www.cincpac.com/afs/testpit.html

This site is maintained by the Archaeological Institute of America at Cornell University. It provides a frequently updated list of opportunities for "hands on" experience in the field of archaeology. Choose a region of the world where you would like to do fieldwork: North America, Mexico, Central America, the Caribbean, the Middle East, Africa, Europe, Asia, Australia, New Zealand and the Pacific, or South America. Within each region are specific locations where fieldwork is being done. The site also gives pertinent information regarding food and lodging, skills required to participate in fieldwork projects, expenses, and the names of people to contact.

Archaeology: An Introduction
http://www.ncl.ac.uk/~nktg/wintro/

This Web site is the electronic companion to Kevin Greene's book, *Archaeology: An Introduction*. Greene, a lecturer in the Department of Archaeology at the University of Newcastle (Tyne, England), offers a list of Internet links supplementing topics in his book. The topics are: (1) The Idea of the Past (2) Discovery, Fieldwork, Recording (3) Excavation (4) Dating the Past (5) Science and Archaeology and (6) Making Sense of the Past. Greene has also compiled a list of additional Internet resources of interest to anthropologists.

Archaeology Magazine
http://www.he.net/~archaeol/

The official journal of the Archaeological Institute of America, *Archaeology Magazine* is one the oldest and most widely circulated scholarly journals of archaeology. The Web site posts news briefs, abstracts, some full-text articles, and a listing of events and museum shows related to archaeology. This is a good resource for persons new to the field of archaeology.

Becoming Involved in Archaeology
http://orca.unl.ac.uk/lamas/lmgetin.htm

The London and Middlesex Archaeology Society prepared the essay "Becoming Involved in Archaeology." In it, the "real" side of archaeology is discussed. Although this essay makes reference to British archaeology, the advice is relevant to anyone interested in pursuing a career or hobby in archaeology. The aim of the article is to explain the rewarding and exciting field of archaeology, while clearing up some common misconceptions about it.

Careers in Archaeology (FAQ)
http://www.museum.state.il.us/ismdepts/anthro/dlcfaq.html

This site, maintained by Texas A&M University, gives answers to some of the most frequently asked questions about careers in archaeology. The questions include: (1) What jobs are available for archaeologists? (2) What education and training are required to become a professional archaeologist? (3) What college or university should I go to? (4) What are some general introductory books on archaeology? (5) I want to go on a dig. How do I volunteer? (6) Where can I get more information on archaeology?

The Current Archaeology Home Page
http://www.compulink.co.uk/~archaeology/cahome.htm

The Current Archaeology Home Page is connected with the British journal, *Current Archaeology*. Check out the link "Council for Independent Archaeology," an organization that promotes the interests of amateur archaeologists. The site also offers career advice and other resources for beginning archaeologists.

The Future of the Past
http://www.cc.ukans.edu/~hoopes/mw/

"The Future of the Past: Archaeology and Anthropology on the World
Wide Web" is a paper written by John W. Hoopes of the Department of
Anthropology and the Museum of Anthropology at the University of
Kansas. In it Hoopes examines "ways that one can use the Web to
enhance research and improve access to a variety of archaeological and
ethnographic materials" held by museum collections.

Guide to Underwater Archaeology Resources on the Internet
http://fiat.gslis.utexas.edu/~trabourn/underwater.html

Tanya R. Raborn (Graduate School of Library and Information Science
at University of Texas–Austin) has posted this "Guide to Underwater
Archaeology Resources on the Internet," which includes information on
organizations, universities, and degree programs; nautical museums;
shipwreck sites; and maritime history and sailing. This Web site also
posts volunteer opportunities for underwater excavation, links to
maritime information, links to underwater archaeology, online
newsletters, electronic discussion lists, and online publications.
Raborn's guide also includes links to: (1) Institutes and Departments of
Underwater Archaeology Organizations (2) Museums and Sites
(3) Maritime History and Sailing (4) Underwater Archaeology Online
(5) SCUBA (the best scuba Internet indices), and (6) Tools for
Underwater Archaeologists.

Health and Safety for Archaeologists
http://seamonkey.ed.asu.edu/swa/health.html

Because archaeologists spend a significant amount of time working
outdoors, it should come as no surprise that they must be prepared to
prevent or treat a range of physical conditions related to sun exposure,
bites and stings, dehydration/water intoxication, and so on. This

Southwest Archaeology Web site explains physical hazards that are prevalent in the southwest part of the United States and offers advice about how to prevent or treat conditions resulting from those hazards.

Increase and Diffusion
http://www.si.edu/i+d/

Increase and Diffusion is a weekly online magazine published by the Smithsonian Institution. Examples of stories include coverage of underwater archaeologist Paul Johnson's dive to the bottom of the sea, the Smithsonian project documenting President Clinton's inauguration, and the Smithsonian acquisition of the Woolworth's lunch counter where 1960s civil rights activists sat to protest segregation and inequality.

Journal of Field Archaeology
http://jfa-www.bu.edu/

The Journal of Field Archaeology is "an international, refereed quarterly journal serving the interests of archaeologists, anthropologists, historians, scientists, and others concerned with the recovery and interpretation of archaeological data. Its scope is worldwide and is not confined to any particular time period." The journal publishes field reports, technical and methodological studies, review articles, occasional general essays, and brief preliminary reports describing fieldwork. The titles and abstracts of the most recent issue and past issues are available at the Web site.

National Association of State Archaeologists
http://www.lib.uconn.edu/NASA/aboutnasa.html

The National Association of State Archaeologists posts a directory of State Archaeologists for the United States and its possessions. Street and e-mail addresses and telephone and fax numbers are listed. State archaeologists can answer questions regarding legal matters, current research, educational programs, or other issues pertaining to archaeology within the state.

NOVA Online/Pyramids—The Inside Story
http://www.pbs.org/wgbh/pages/nova/pyramid/

This site contains many pictures and maps and it is best viewed with Netscape. It is dedicated to the story of the pyramids. You can be part of Khufu, Khafre, Menkaure, and the Sphinx pyramid excavations, read interviews with archaeologists, and view photographs and maps.

NOVA also gives access to transcripts from its "This Old Pyramid" broadcasts on Stonehenge, Inca, Obelisk and Colosseum.

Palaeolithic Cave Paintings
http://www.culture.fr/culture/arcnat/chauvet/en/gvpda-d.htm

The French Ministry of Culture has posted photographs and descriptions of the discovery of Palaeolithic cave paintings in the Ardèche gorges (southern France). This site documents the discovery of the cave, the excavation process and the significance of this finding to the archaeological community.

Papers from the Institute of Archaeology
http://www.ucl.ac.uk/archaeology/pia/

"Papers from the Institute of Archaeology (PIA) was launched in 1990 by a group of research students at the Institute of Archaeology, University College London" with the goal of providing an "outlet for research at the graduate level." Selected back issues of this journal are available online, while others are available for purchase. Each online issue contains the full text of articles, book reviews, and abstracts of archaeology dissertations. Of particular interest are "The Problems and Prospects of Cultural Evolution" (Issue 1) and "Mortuary Practices among the Aztecs in the Light of Ethnohistorical and Archaeological Sources" (Issue 4).

Protecting Archaeological Sites Today (P.A.S.T)
http:// home.uleth.ca/geo/jasweb/jasweb.htm

Protecting Archaeological Sites Today (P.A.S.T) was created January 2, 1997, with the purpose of becoming a clearinghouse for information on "the preservation of archaeological, cultural, and historic sites, through political action and education." This organization seeks to preserve places threatened by corporate development, government actions, or other kinds of destructive behavior. There is a form to complete if you wish to list a site that is in such danger.

Quaternary Sciences Center Research Areas, Desert Research Institute
http://www.dri.edu/QSC/Research_Areas.html#AppEnv

This site, provided by the Desert Research Institute, is divided into six anthropological-and archaeological-related subsections: anthropological and archaeological research, geomorphology, applied environmental studies, palaeoenvironmental research, quaternary chronology, and palaeoecology and palaeoclimatology. Although some of the subsections have intimidating titles, the Desert Research Institute gives a clear description of each.

SAAweb—Society for American Archaeology
http://www.saa.org/

The Society for American Archaeology, founded in 1934, has more than 5,600 members who are "dedicated to the research, interpretation, and protection of the archaeological heritage of the Americas." At this site you can find information related to membership, publications, conferences, bylaws, and other archaeological information. Of particular interest to students are an answer to the question "What is archaeology?", an overview of career opportunities in archaeology, the document, Principles of Archaeological Ethics; and the Society for American Archaeology Bulletin. The Bulletin contains interesting articles, essays, and news. Examples from the November 1996 issue include "9,300-Year-Old Skeleton Sparks Controversy in Northwest," "Working Together—The Archaeological Field Schools in the 1990s," and "Student Affairs—Getting Graphics! Making an Effective Poster."

Sierra Club Policy: Archaeological Sites
http://www.sierraclub.org/policy/411.html

This site lists the Sierra Club's official policy on archaeological sites. It begins, "Archaeological resources are the material result of past human activity. These irreplaceable resources include, but are not limited to, artifacts, campsites, villages, dwellings, earth works, and rock art."

The Society for Historical Archaeology
http://www.azstarnet.com/~sha/

The Society for Historical Archaeology (SHA), formed in 1967, is "the largest scholarly group concerned with the archaeology of the modern world (1400-present)." The society is specifically concerned with "the identification, excavation, interpretation, and conservation of sites and materials on land and underwater" and supports "the conservation, preservation and research of archaeological resources, including both land and underwater remains." This site offers contents and abstracts of current issues of the *Historical Archaeology Journal* and access to the society's newsletter. There is an excellent link for "Kids!" that explores the field of archaeology, career opportunities, and rewards of choosing archaeology as a profession.

US Cultural Protection Legislation
http://www.lib.uconn.edu/ArchNet/Topical/CRM/crmusdoc.html

The University of Connecticut Library offers access to "federal
legislation related to historic preservation and cultural resource
management" including the Organic Act of 1916, the National Historic
Preservation Act of 1966, the Archaeological Resources Protection Act
of 1979, and the Native American Grave Protection and Repatriation
Act of 1990.

Vermillion Accord on Human Remains
http://wac.soton.ac.uk/wac/ethics/vermillion.accord.html

The World Archaeological Congress (WAC) offers an international
discussion forum for anyone "genuinely concerned with the study of
the past." WAC seeks "to recognize the historical and social role and
political context of archaeology," and strives to "make archaeological
studies relevant to the wider community." This site contains the
Vermillion Accord on Human Remains, adopted by WAC in 1989,
which relates to the use and care of human remains.

World Archaeological Congress—Code of Ethics
http://wac.soton.ac.uk/wac/ethics/ethics.html

"First Code of Ethics and Principles" governing archaeological
research and inquiry are posted. This code recognizes that
archaeologists have obligations to indigenous people, and it offers eight
principles and seven rules that they should follow. The World
Archaeological Congress Code of Ethics was inspired by the 1989
Vermillion Accord on Human Remains.

Arctic

Arctic Circle
http://www.lib.uconn.edu/ArcticCircle

The goal of Arctic Circle is to stimulate "interest in the peoples and
environment of the Arctic and Subarctic region" with special emphasis
and excellent resources on natural resources, history and culture, social
equity, and environmental justice. Be sure to check out "Euro-
American Portrayal" of those who "explored" the Arctic and
"Indigenous Responses" to their presence. Also of interest is
"Ethnographic Portraits" of Arctic and Subarctic Peoples.

Arctic Research Consortium of the U.S.
http://arcus.polarnet.com/Home.htm

The Arctic Research Consortium of the United States (ARCUS) was established in 1989 with the goal of understanding "the physical, chemical, biological, and social processes of the arctic system that interact with the total Earth system and thus contribute to or are influenced by global change." Probably the most useful information for those new to arctic research is "Selected Education Links," a list of links to Internet resources on the arctic.

Arctic Studies Center
http://nmnhwww.si.edu/arctic/

The Arctic Studies Center of the Smithsonian Institution "is devoted to the study of arctic peoples, cultures and environments." There are links to feature exhibitions, research, and other exhibitions. Two excellent essays are available online: "Traditional Ecological Knowledge" (TEK) as it applies to beluga whales and "DNA Research" as it applies to the people of Siberia.

Ethnographic Portraits (Of Arctic and Subarctic Peoples)
http://www.lib.uconn.edu/ArcticCircle/CulturalViability/portraits.
html

These portraits include "An Introduction to Northern Peoples," "The Crees of Northern Quebec," "The Inupiat of Arctic Alaska," "The Nenets and Khanty of Yamal Peninsula, Northwest Siberia," "The Sami of Far Northern Europe," and "Greenland: a Modern Arctic Society."

Arts

African Art: Aesthetics and Meaning
http://www.lib.virginia.edu/dic/exhib/93.ray.aa/African.html

This site contains "a catalog of an exhibition of African art at the Bayly Museum, University of Virginia." The purpose of this exhibit is to examine the "formal aesthetic aspects of the objects and the moral and religious ideas they express." This site includes an introductory guide explaining the meaning and "elements of African aesthetics," as well as an online exhibition of African art. For each exhibit, there is a brief description focusing on the aesthetic value and meaning of the piece and on the materials used to create the piece. Included in the description is information on the region of Africa from which the artwork originated. This site must be viewed using Netscape.

African Art Gallery
http://www.afrinet.net/gallery

This site is maintained by AfriNET Gallery whose mission is to provide "the finest and most comprehensive collection of African American, Caribbean and African Art available today." This site includes "original art, graphics (traditional printmaking techniques such as serigraphy, lithography and etching), fine art prints, posters, sculptures, and mixed media." This site is best viewed using Netscape.

Asian Art Museum of San Francisco
http://www.asianart.org/

The Asian Art Museum of San Francisco, founded in 1959, offers the online exhibit "Mongolia: The Legacy of Genghis Khan. This exhibition highlights the Mongolian renaissance, an era that began in the sixteenth-century with the Mongols' attempt to recreate the empire that had flourished under Genghis Khan three hundred years earlier." This site must be viewed using Netscape.

Brooklyn Museum of Art
http://wwar.com/brooklyn_museum/index.html

The Brooklyn Museum of Art posts a variety of online exhibits including Egyptian, Classical and Ancient Middle Eastern, the Arts of Africa and the Pacific, the Americas, and Asia. This site must be viewed using Netscape.

Nok—The Museum of African Art @Harlemm
http://harlemm.com/nokbeta/

The Nok Museum of African Arts is a virtual museum "dedicated to the study, preservation, and exhibition of all forms of African art and its derivatives." The museum maintains "an electronic collection of works held by other museums and private collectors." This site is best viewed using Netscape.

Palaeolithic cave paintings
http://www.culture.fr/culture/arcnat/chauvet/en/gvpda-d.htm

The French Ministry of Culture has posted photographs and descriptions of the discovery of Palaeolithic cave paintings in the Ardèche gorges (southern France). This site documents the discovery of the cave, the excavation process and the importance and significance of this finding to the archaeological community.

Asia

American Oriental Society
http://www-personal.umich.edu/~jrodgers/

The American Oriental Society, maintained by the University of Michigan, encourages "basic research in the languages and literature of Asia." The table of contents for the most recent *Journal of the American Oriental Society* and for the society's newsletter is available. The newsletter can be downloaded. The most useful information for students is the Proposed Guidelines for Professional Ethics for the American Oriental Society.

Asia
http://sunsite.berkeley.edu/

The Librarians' Index to the Internet includes the category "Asia." Select that category and find links to Web sites such as "China News Digest," "Japan Resources," and "Top News from Asia."

Asian Art Museum of San Francisco
http://www.asianart.org/

The Asian Art Museum of San Francisco, founded in 1959, offers the online exhibit "Mongolia: The Legacy of Genghis Khan. This exhibition highlights the Mongolian renaissance, an era that began in the sixteenth-century with the Mongols' attempt to recreate the empire that had flourished under Genghis Khan three hundred years earlier." This site must be viewed using Netscape.

Asian Studies WWW Virtual Library
http://coombs.anu.edu.au/WWWVL-AsianStudies.html/

The Australian National University "provides an authoritative, continuously updated" guide to information on the Internet related to the "Asian continent as a whole, as well as individual Asian regions, countries, and territories." The Asian Studies WWW Virtual Library is a multinational, collaborative effort that draws on the expertise of 32 editors from 13 countries.

The Association for Asian Studies
http://www.aasianst.org

The Association for Asian Studies "is open to all persons interested in Asia" and seeks to increase exchange of information and understanding of East, South, and Southeast Asia." Abstracts of papers presented or to be presented at 1995, 1996, and 1997 AAS annual meetings are available online. Current and back issues of the *Asian Studies Newsletter* are also available.

Cultural Bridge Productions
http://www.culturalbridge.com/

This Web site, sponsored by Cultural Bridge Productions, allows you to "explore some of the world's cultures through provocative, opinionated travelogues and interviews." From this site, read about specific cultures in a variety of countries including China, South Korea, Japan and Vietnam. As one example of the kind of material on this site, consider that upon choosing Japan, the following documents (and more) can be accessed: "A Long Way Home: Growing up Nisei in Japan During the Pacific War," "School Days in Japan: Photos from the Yamamoto Hinako Album," "Notes from a Japanese Travel Journal (parts 1 and 2)," and "Japanese Valentine's Days." This site is best viewed using Netscape.

Top 10 News from Asia
http://www.asianmall.com/top10news/

Top 10 News from Asia covers business, political, and social issues in Asia. From this site, search newspapers and magazines for specific information, or browse through "Today's Top News," "Jobs in Asia," "Weather Outlook," and "News Archives."

Caribbean

Caribbean Cultural Center/African Diaspora Institute
http://www.igc.org/caribctr/

"The Franklin H. Williams Caribbean Cultural Center/ African Diaspora Institute is a unique arts and cultural organization that celebrates, documents, and shares the rich cultural heritage and vibrant spiritual and creative expressions of people of African descent throughout the world, particularly of the Caribbean and Central, South, and North America. Since 1976, it has been dedicated to opening and sustaining an ongoing dialogue about the cultures and communities of the African diaspora." From this site, you may view the current exhibition of the art gallery, as well as order items from the Center's gift shop.

Codes of Ethics

The Belmont Report
http://www.ncgr.org/gpi/odyssey/privacy/Belmt.html

The U.S. Department of Health, Education, and Welfare posts the *Belmont Report: Ethical Principles and Guidelines for the Protection of Human Subjects of Research* prepared by the National Commission for the Protection of Human Subjects. The report is "a statement of basic ethical principles and guidelines that should assist in resolving the ethical problems that surround the conduct of research with human subjects."

American Anthropological Association Code of Ethics
http://www.ameranthassn.org/ethics.htm

The American Anthropological Association "Ethics" section provides the draft *AAA Code of Ethics,* the *Final Report of the Commission to Revise the AAA Statements on Ethics*, and *the AAA Casebook on Ethical Issues in Anthropology.* The casebook reprints Ethical Dilemmas originally published in the *Anthropology Newsletter* in the 1970s and 1980s. The AAA also gives links to other associations and their codes of ethics (e.g. American Political Science Association, American Psychological Association, National Association of Social Workers).

NAGPRA Documentation by Category
http://www.cast.uark.edu/other/nps/nagpra/

The Center for Advanced Spatial Technologies (CAST) at the University of Arkansas has placed on the Internet documents related to the Native American Graves Protection and Repatriation Act. The documents are sorted according to four categories: "Legal Mandates," "Guidance," "Notices," and "Review Committee." Full text of all documents is available online.

NAGPRA GUIDANCE: List of Tribal, Native Alaskan Entity, and Native Hawaiian
http://www.cast.uark.edu/other/nps/nagpra/nagpra.dat/gid003.html

This site outlines the Native American Graves Protection and Repatriation Act (NAGPRA) signed by President Bush in 1990. "The statute requires Federal agencies and museums that receive Federal funds to consult with Indian tribes, Native Alaskan entities, and Native Hawaiian organizations regarding the proper care and disposition of Native American human remains, funerary objects, sacred objects, and objects of cultural patrimony."

Vermillion Accord on Human Remains
http://wac.soton.ac.uk/wac/ethics/vermillion.accord.html

The World Archaeological Congress (WAC) offers an international discussion forum for anyone "genuinely concerned with the study of the past." WAC seeks "to recognize the historical and social role and political context of archaeology," and strives to "make archaeological studies relevant to the wider community." This site contains the Vermillion Accord on Human Remains, adopted by WAC in 1989, which relates to the treatment and care of human remains.

World Archaeological Congress—Code of Ethics
http://wac.soton.ac.uk/wac/ethics/ethics.html

The "First Code of Ethics and Principles" governing archaeological research and inquiry is posted at this site. This code recognizes that archaeologists have obligations to indigenous people, and it offers eight principles and seven rules that they should follow. The World Archaeological Congress Code of Ethics was inspired by the 1989 Vermillion Accord on Human Remains.

Congressional Activities of Interest to Anthropologists

Cover Stories from Previous Congressional Quarterly Weekly Report Stories
http://www.cq.com/wr.htm

From this site it's possible to read the cover stories from the *Congressional Quarterly Weekly* for any week in the previous year. Use the search engine to find stories related to anthropological issues.

Penny Hill Press
http://www.clark.net/pub/pennyhill

Penny Hill Press offers "same-day shipment of all publications of the Congressional Research Service (CRS), the 741 person, $62 million-per-year 'think tank' that works exclusively for members and committees of the United States Congress. Subscribers of the monthly *Congressional Research Report* get same-day shipment of any of more than 1,000 studies and other publications produced by CRS for $3 each, with a minimum order of documents." Students may receive these reports for $17 per item. This site offers abstracts of CRS reports on a variety of subjects ranging from abortion to women's issues. Since it is likely that your public or university library subscribes to CRR, use this site to search for material before going to the library. For abstracts on specific geographic regions of the world use the following endings to the URL listed above:

Middle East or North African countries	**/publpennyhill/mideast.html**
Africa	**/publpennyhill/africa.html**
Americas	**/publpennyhill/americas.html**
Asia	**/publpennyhill/asia.html**
Europe	**/publpennyhill/europe.html**

THOMAS: Legislative Information on the Internet
http://thomas.loc.gov/

This site is an attempt to make federal legislative information freely available to the Internet public. "Hot Topics" are those bills and amendments that are subjects of floor action, debate, and hearings in Congress and that are frequently reported on by the popular media. You can search by topic for the most up-to-date information on legislation related to issues of concern to anthropologists (language, culture, and race). From this site it is possible to read the full text of bills and find out who sponsored and cosponsored them.

Country Information (General)

Background Notes on the Countries of the World
http://www.state.gov/www/background_notes/index.html

This site contains statistical and general information on most of the countries of the world (but not the United States) and covers geography, people, education, economics, and membership in international organizations.

Country Studies
http://lcweb2.loc.gov/frd/cs/country.html

This site gives access to book-length information on Ethiopia, China, Egypt, Indonesia, Israel, Japan, Philippines, Singapore, Somalia, South Korea, and Yugoslavia. It is a comprehensive source of information about all areas of life including politics, economics, religion, population, history, and culture.

Country Studies/Area Handbook Program
http://lcweb2.loc.gov/frd/cs/cshome.html

The Country Studies/Area Handbook Program is an ongoing and continuously updated series of books prepared by the Federal Research Division of the Library of Congress. There are 71 country studies online. Each country study gives a comprehensive overview of the society, geography, economy, politics, history, people, and major institutions (religion, education, and medicine).

International Demographic Data
http://www.census.gov/ftp/pub/ipc/www/idbsum.html

This Census Bureau site includes data on the population of every country and territory in the world for 1950, 1960, 1970, 1980, 1990, and 1991-1995. Population is also projected to the year 2000, as is age-specific population.

The World Factbook 1996
http://www.odci.gov/cia/publications/nsolo/factbook/global.htm#W

This 1996 CIA World Factbook includes a section that considers the world as a unit. For example, it gives the unemployment rate, population size, total fertility, and so on for the world.

U.S. Department of State Home Page
http://www.state.gov/

This site is an official U.S. Government source. The U.S. Department of State is the main U.S. foreign affairs agency and is responsible for implementing the President's foreign policies. The Hot Spot link updates you on most recent spotlighted information concerning foreign policies, such as "Patterns of Global Terrorism" and "Earth Day." The travel link gives you information on every area in the world and the traveling requirements to get there. This site also gives useful telephone numbers and a 1996 Department Telephone Directory.

Cultural Anthropology

African Art: Aesthetics and Meaning
http://www.lib.virginia.edu/dic/exhib/93.ray.aa/African.html

This site contains "a catalog of an exhibition of African art at the Bayly Museum, University of Virginia." The purpose of this exhibit is to examine the "formal aesthetic aspects of the objects and the moral and religious ideas they express." This site includes an introductory guide explaining the meaning and "elements of African aesthetics," as well as an online exhibition of African art. For each exhibit, there is a brief description focusing on the aesthetic value and meaning of the piece and on the materials used to create the piece. Included in the description is information on the region of Africa from which the artwork originated. This site must be viewed using Netscape.

African Art Gallery
http://www.afrinet.net/gallery

This site is maintained by AfriNET Gallery whose mission is to provide "the finest and most comprehensive collection of African American, Caribbean and African Art available today." This site includes "original art, graphics (traditional printmaking techniques such as serigraphy, lithography and etching), fine art prints, posters, sculptures and mixed media." This site is best viewed using Netscape.

American Ethnologist
http://www.ameranthassn.org/aespubs.htm

American Ethnologist is a quarterly journal produced by the American Ethnological Society, a division of the AAA. This site gives access to the journal's contents including abstracts. The journal publishes ethnographic research in the broadest sense of the term. Studying the abstracts and titles offers insights about the ethnographic approach to studying human groups and societies and may help you generate ideas for your own ethnographic research. For example, the November 1996 (Volume 23, No. 4) issue includes papers on (1) a Corsican spelling contest as an effort to promote a minority language (2) the words and actions characteristic of the staff and residents at a shelter for the mentally ill and homeless, and (3) the process by which groups struggle to claim, define, and give meaning to culturally significant public spaces.

American Folklore Society
http://gopher.panam.edu:70/1gopher_root10%3a%5b000000%5d

The *American Folklore Society Newsletter* publishes interesting articles and information. Unfortunately the newsletters are long, and there is no table of contents so you have to browse each one to see what they contain. However, if you have to do general research on folklore, the time you take to browse the newsletters will be useful.

The Anthropologist in the Field
http://www.truman.edu/academics/ss/faculty/tamakoshi/index.html

Laura Tamakoshi and Brian Cross at Truman State University prepared this guide to fieldwork research. It has 4 major sections: (1) planning (2) method (3) writing, and (4) reference. Each of these four sections has several subsections. For example the planning section includes information regarding proposals, preparation, choosing a field site, and travel arrangements.

Asian Art Museum of San Francisco
http://www.asianart.org/

The Asian Art Museum of San Francisco, founded in 1959, offers the online exhibit "Mongolia: The Legacy of Genghis Khan. This exhibition highlights the Mongolian renaissance, an era that began in the sixteenth century with the Mongol's attempt to recreate the empire that had flourished under Genghis Khan three hundred years earlier." This site must be viewed using Netscape.

Brooklyn Museum of Art
http://wwar.com/brooklyn_museum/index.html

The Brooklyn Museum of Art posts a variety of online exhibits including Egyptian, Classical and Ancient Middle Eastern Art, as well as the Arts of Africa and the Pacific, the Americas, and Asia. This site must be viewed using Netscape.

Center for Social Anthropology and Computing (CSAC)
http://lucy.ukc.ac.uk

The University of Kent at Canterbury sponsors the CSAS Web site. CSAS aims to serve the worldwide anthropology community and to advance anthropology by offering information resources, developing new methods for researching anthropological problems, and promoting the use of computer technology in anthropological research. Of particular interest on this Web site is the CSAC Studies in Anthropology Vol. 11, which offers full text of various anthropological papers including such topics as "Indigenous Knowledge of the Rainforest" and "City Dweller Perceptions of African Forests." These papers can be accessed directly at **http://lucy.ukc.ac.uk/CSACSIA/Research.html**. Also included in this document is the text of papers sponsored by the CSAC. Manuscripts include "Kinship, Marriage and Residence—A Database Approach" which describes how computers have assisted anthropologists studying complex subjects such as kinship. This paper may be accessed directly at **http://lucy.ukc.ac.uk:80/CSACSIA/Vol11/Papers/index.html**.

CAM—Cultural Anthropology Methods
http://www.lawrence.edu/~bradleyc/cam.html

The journal *Cultural Anthropology Methods* publishes articles related to qualitative and quantitative methods in anthropology. The table of contents for all issues of CAM published since 1989 is online. Three sample articles are available. One is on ethnographic sampling; a second is about cross-cultural research, and a third is a Guttman scale analysis of Matsigenka Men's Manufacturing Skills.

Cultural Exchange
http://deil.lang.uiuc.edu/exchange/

Cultural Exchange is a University of Illinois, Urbana-Champaign, electronic publication that welcomes submissions of 2,000 words or less from non-native English speakers from around the world. This publication includes essays in which authors describe some aspect of their culture (a graduation ceremony, a ritual, a holiday celebration, a tradition), react to news events in their country, submit a short story, or present a poem. Although the primary goal of *Exchange* is to support a forum for non-native English speakers to express themselves in English, the journal is also a unique resource for English speakers interested in culture.

Culture of the Net   (Research on)
http://www.vianet.net.au/~timn/thesis/index.html

This anthropology masters thesis by Tim North is an excellent example of ethnographic research. North argues that a new culture has emerged from the ever-growing population of Internet users and that the Internet has become a society with its own distinct culture. He describes that culture, emphasizing its impact on newcomers and the process by which they become enculturated. North presents more than the end product of his ethnographic research. He describes each step of the research process, explaining how he did his research. This is helpful for those doing their first research proposal or literature review, or those who need advice about how to gain entree, take notes, or write up research results.

Cultural Perspectives on Food and Nutrition
http://www.nal.usda.gov/fnic/pubs/bibs/gen/cultural.html

The National Agriculture Library prepared the Special Research Brief (SRB-94-03), "Cultural Perspectives on Food and Nutrition." It is a bibliography with abstracts divided into three sections—General, Educational, and Research. Examples of titles include "Body Images, Body-Size Perceptions, and Eating Behaviors Among African-American and White College Students;" "America Eats Out: Illustrated History of Restaurants, Taverns, Coffee Shops, Speakeasies, and Other Establishments that Have Fed Us for 350 Years;" "Bibliography and Sourcebook on Seventh-Day Adventists' Work With Soyfoods, Vegetarianism, and Wheat Gluten, 1866-1992"; and "Nutritional Requirements of The Elderly: A Japanese View." The bibliography and abstracts offer excellent overviews of the relationship between food, diet, and nutrition and culture.

Cultural Studies and Critical Theory
http://eng.hss.cmu.edu/theory/

Cultural Studies and Critical Theory is a multidisciplinary journal that publishes research about contemporary texts and cultural practices. It welcomes submissions from those in a broad range of disciplines including anthropology, sociology, gender studies, feminism, literary criticism, history, and psychoanalysis. As a way of introducing readers to the field of cultural studies and critical theory, there are dozens of manuscripts online including the following titles: "Alien Abductions and the End of White People," "The Allure of Ethnic Eateries," "TV Heroines & Money Anonymous," "Writing, Knowledge and Postmodern Anthropology," and "The World of Coca-Cola."

Descriptions of 57 Religions, Faith Groups & Ethical Systems
http://web.canlink.com/ocrt/var_rel.htm

As the title suggests this Web site offers descriptions of 57 religions, faith groups, and ethical systems. The 57 descriptions are broken down into the following categories: 1) Long established major world religions (e.g., Buddhism, Judaism, and Christianity) 2) Small, non-Christian religions (e.g., Hare Krishna and Unitarian Universalism) 3) Destructive faith groups (e.g., The Family and Branch Dividians) 4) Other; and 5) Other ethical groups, religions, and spiritual paths. This Web site is supported by the Ontario Consultants on Religious Tolerance whose aims are to promote tolerance of minority religions, offer useful information on controversial religious topics, and expose hatred and misinformation about any religion.

Ethnographic Portraits (Of Arctic and Subarctic Peoples)
http://www.lib.uconn.edu/ArcticCircle/culturalviability/portraits.html

Ethnographic Portraits is part of Arctic Circle. The portraits include "An Introduction to Northern Peoples," "The Crees of Northern Quebec," "The Inupiat of Arctic Alaska," "The Nenets and Khanty of Yamal Peninsula, Northwest Siberia," "The Sami of Far Northern Europe," and "Greenland: a Modern Arctic Society."

Family History Library
http://www.genhomepage.com/LDS.html

"The Church of Jesus Christ of Latter-Day Saints (LDS church) runs the Family History Library (FHL) in Salt Lake City, Utah. The FHL has one of the most impressive collections of genealogical material in the world." This site gives access to the addresses and home pages of various Family History Centers throughout the U.S. In addition, the FHL offers access to online databases such as the Social Security Death Index, the U.S. Colonial Vital Index, and the American Marriage Record.

Folklife and Fieldwork (Guide)
http://lcweb.loc.gov/folklife/fieldwk.html

The American Folklife Center gives online access to a folklife fieldwork guide, *A Layman's Introduction to Field Techniques,* by Peer Bartes. There is a brief introduction to folklife followed by a review of a fieldwork project in three parts: 1) preparation 2) fieldwork itself, and 3) processing the material collected.

The Genealogy Home Page
http://www.genhomepage.com/full.html

Genealogy Roots Corner is the organization that sponsors The Genealogy Home Page. "The goal of Genealogy Roots Corner is to gather researchers together on one site" to share information that will help others searching for missing branches of the family tree and seeking to make family connections. This is an excellent comprehensive "library" of information on the Internet including (1) Genealogy Guides (2) Libraries (3) Maps, Geography, Deeds and Photography (4) Newsgroups and Mailing Lists (5) Genealogy Societies (6) World Wide Genealogy Resources, and much more. There are more than 1600 links to Internet resources.

Getting Started in Oral Tradition Research—A Manual
http://tailpipe.learnnet.nt.ca/pwnhc/

The Prince of Wales Northern Heritage Centre supports the **Gwich'in** Social and Cultural Institute (GSC). The Institute documents **Gwich'**in oral history and traditional knowledge. A manual outlining the basic principles of oral tradition research has been posted. The manual defines oral tradition, written tradition, and traditional knowledge. It also gives advice on preparing for interviews, interviewing, processing information, and reporting results.

Journal of the Society for Cultural Anthropology
http://www.pitzer.edu/~cultanth/frmain.htm

Cultural Anthropology, the journal of the Society for Cultural Anthropology, "welcomes contributions of relevance to cultural studies broadly conceived." Contents (titles only) of the most recent issue and past issues are available.

Kinship Tutorial, Main Menu
http://www.umanitoba.ca/anthropology/tutor/kinmenu.html

This excellent kinship tutorial was prepared by Brian Schwimmer, Department of Anthropology, University of Manitoba. The link "Kinship Fundamentals" begins the tutorial. Other links include systems of descent, kinship terminology, marriage systems, and residence rules. Three ethnographic cases help to bring kinship concepts to life. Those cases are a Turkish peasant village, the Yanomano of the Amazon Forest, and ancient Hebrews.

Life History Manuscripts from the Folklore Project
http://lcweb2.loc.gov/wpaintro/wpahome.html

Life History Manuscripts from the Folklore Project was a product of the Works Progress Administration (WPA). The federal government established the WPA in the 1930s to give employment to those who could not find work during the Depression. Specifically, the WPA Federal Writers' Project (1936-1940) gave work to unemployed writers or to anyone who could qualify as a writer. Approximately 300 writers from 24 states interviewed people across the country from all walks of life and circumstances. The product of their efforts was a collection containing 2,900 documents ranging from 2,000 to 15,000 words. The collection can be searched by keywords (such as textile workers, immigrants, or ex-slaves) and according to region or state.

Myths and Legends
http://pubpages.unh.edu/%7Ecbsiren/myth.html

Christopher Siren, a graduate student in physics at the University of New Hampshire, has created a virtual encyclopedia of links to Web sites on the WWW related to myths and legends. Siren organizes his links by culture area (e.g., Greek and Roman, Slavic and Baltic, Native American, African). For example, the link to "African story lines" explains the Ashanti myth of "Anasi the Spider-man" and traces its path through African and Western mythology, and the link "Bigfoot legends" explores the legend of Bigfoot in Native American folklore.

Nok—The Museum of African Art @Harlemm
http://harlemm.com/nokbeta/

The Nok Museum of African Arts is a virtual museum "dedicated to the study, preservation and exhibition of all forms of African arts and its derivatives." The museum maintains "an electronic collection of works held by other museums and private collectors." This site is best viewed using Netscape.

Palaeolithic Cave Paintings
http://www.culture.fr/culture/arcnat/chauvet/en/gvpda-d.htm

The French Ministry of Culture has posted photographs and descriptions of the discovery of Palaeolithic cave paintings in the Ardèche gorges (southern France). This site documents the discovery of the cave, the excavation process and the importance and significance of this finding to the archaeological community.

Qualitative Research in Information Systems
http://www.aukland.ac.nz/msis/isworld/

This site provides an excellent overview of qualitative research for those students interested in learning about its methods and applications. It begins with a comparison between qualitative and quantitative research methods and offers a basic definition of triangulation (an approach to social research that combines quantitative and qualitative research). The emphasis is on the methods of qualitative research: case study research, critical social theory, ethnographic research, grounded theory and interpretive research, narrative and metaphor, and actions research. For each method, you will find a brief definition and a list of selected references for further reading.

Religious and Sacred Texts
http://Web pages.marshall.edu/~wiley6/rast.htmlx

The Religious and Sacred Texts Web site compiles links to various texts and resources on the Internet to help interested parties explore the history, thoughts, and writings of various religions from around the world. Categories listed include Apocryphal texts, Islamic texts, Hindu texts, the Analects of Confucius, Mormon texts, Taoist texts, World Scripture, Bahai texts, Sikh texts, The Egyptian Book of the Dead, Gnostic texts, Zen texts, texts by Early Christian Fathers, Zoroastrian texts, Divrei Torah, the Urantia Book, Ethiopian texts, and medieval texts.

Shamanism—Frequently Asked Questions (FAQ)
http://lucy.ukc.ac.uk/cgi-bin/makehtml?Papers/shaman_FAQ

This site gives a general overview on the subject of Shamanism by answering ten frequently asked questions including "What is Shamanism?" and "What is Shamanic Ecstasy?" There is also information on "Becoming a Shaman," "The Role of Trauma in the Development of a Shaman," "The Relationship Between Shamanic Traditions and Culture," "The Role of Shamanic Ecstasy," "The Origin of the Term Shamanism," and "Roles of the Shaman."

USGenWeb Project
http://www.usgenweb.com/

The USGenWeb Project is a not-for-profit organization with the goal of making "genealogical research material available through the Internet, ranging from various biographies to county vital records (birth, death, marriage), etc." Links to Internet sites are categorized according to the following levels: world, United States, and individual states. At the state level there are links to Web sites that give access to vital records, surname searches, and links to other genealogical resources.

Web of Culture
http://www.worldculture.com/

E. F. Sheridan, president of The Web of Culture and also an independent consultant, developed this Web site for a graduate course in cross-cultural communications. This site offers information useful to those about to travel abroad, as well as to those who are interested in learning more about customs and practices in other cultures. Some topics covered include gestures (did you know that the "ok" hand gesture in America is considered an obscene gesture in Spain?), currency (including exchange rates), holidays and international headlines. There is also a language link which allows you to identify the language(s) you speak and the one you want to learn. The computer displays common words and phrases in your native language and gives a translation in the language you want to learn. If you have specific questions about a culture, this site includes a "Cultural Contact" which allows you to pose your questions directly to a "native" of that culture using e-mail.

World Cultures
http://sunsite.berkeley.edu/

The Librarians' Index to the Internet includes the category "World Cultures." Select that category and find links to Web sites such as "Association of Gypsies," "Gypsy Lore Society," and "Immigration and Multicultural Studies."

WorldGenWeb
http://www.dsenter.com/worldgenweb/index.html

The WorldGenWeb Project is maintained in conjunction with the USGenWeb Project, a not-for-profit organization with the goal of making "genealogical research material available through the Internet, ranging from various biographies to county vital records (birth, death, marriage), etc." This site offers links to Web pages offering genealogical information based in countries ranging from Afghanistan to Zimbabwe.

World Lecture Hall—Anthropology
http://www.utexas.edu/world/lecture/ant

"The World Lecture Hall (WLH) contains links to pages created by faculty worldwide who are using the Web to deliver class materials. For example, you will find course syllabi, assignments, lecture notes, exams, class calendars, multimedia, textbooks, etc." This site contains information about online anthropology courses including "Anthropology, Cyberspace and the Internet," "Cultural Anthropology," "Cultures and Cures," and "Cultures in Contact."

World Scripture: A Comparative Anthology of Sacred Texts
http://www.rain.org/~origin/ws.html

The International Religious Foundation is an organization dedicated to promoting world peace through interreligious dialogue and cooperation. Select "Introduction" for more information on the purpose of the project. The foundation has posted the scriptures of several of the major world religions according to how each religion views (1) ultimate reality (2) divine law, truth, and cosmic principles (3) the purpose of human life (4) life beyond death, and (5) the human condition, as well as 16 other topics.

Cyber Anthropology

What is Cyber Anthropology?
http://www.clas.ufl.edu/users/seeker1/cyberanthro/newhome.html

The Department of Anthropology, University of Florida, defines *Cyber Anthropology,* as "the study of humans in virtual communities and networked environments." Visit this Web site for a comprehensive definition and overview of this new subspecialty.

Developmental Anthropology

Annual Editions: Developing World
http://www.dushkin.com/annualeditions/0-697-36333-3.mhtml

This site offers abstracts to 44 articles reprinted in *Annual Editions: Developing Worlds*. Simply reading the abstracts gives an excellent overview of the kinds of topics of interest to developmental anthropologists.

Center for Civil Society International (CCSI)
http://solar.rtd.utk.edu/~ccsi/ccsihome.html

The highest priority of Seattle-based Center for Civil Society International (CCSI) is to publicize "creative collaborations between voluntary organizations in the U.S. and the West and new third sector organizations emerging in the New Independent States" of the former Soviet Union. Examples of third sector organizations include Psychological Crisis Center for Women and the American Chamber of

Commerce in Russia. This is a bilingual Web site with more than 2,000 documents and links to relevant Internet sites. In addition, this site offers electronic archives of CCSI's newsletter, *Civil Society: East and West*, as well as other CCSI publications.

Charity Organizations
http://www.charity.org/

This site is maintained by the International Service Agencies (ISA) with the primary mission of helping "millions of people overseas and in the United States who suffer from hunger, poverty, and disease or from the ravages of war, oppression, and natural disasters." This site contains a list of the 54 member agencies of ISA. Select an agency and access the corresponding home page. Examples of charity organizations referenced include American Refugees Committee, AmeriCare, Doctors Without Borders, Near East Foundation, and World Relief Corporation.

U.S. Agency for International Development
http://www.info.usaid.gov/

The U.S. Agency for International Development, known as USAID, is an independent government agency that provides economic development and humanitarian assistance in order to advance U.S. economic and political interests overseas. This site contains information on USAID's record of accomplishments, its *1995 Agency Performance Report*, and policy papers. There are also articles explaining the importance of foreign aid, the meaning of participatory development, and strategies for sustainable development. See also the "Lessons Without Borders" link, which seeks to share with readers lessons learned overseas.

Volunteers in Technical Assistance
http://www.vita.org/

Volunteers in Technical Assistance (VITA) is an organization that provides information services to people living in developing countries so that they can draw upon it to improve the quality of their lives. VITA "collects, refines, and disseminates information such as that necessary to improve food production, minister health needs, increase productivity of businesses, generate higher incomes, and preserve natural resources." Read descriptions of VITA projects in Benin, Guinea, the Central African Republic, Madagascar, and Chad. VITA also posts its monthly newsletter *Develop Net* which covers online news and views related to technology transfers. Example of new stories include: "Is There a Water Shortage?," "Distance Education in the Caribbean," and "Investing in Electricity in Latin America" (see January 1997 issue).

The World Bank Group
http://www.worldbank.org/

The World Bank Group is made up of five organizations: the International Bank for Reconstruction and Development [IBRD], the International Development Association [IDA], the International Finance Corporation [IRC], the Multilateral Investment Guarantee Agency [MIGA], and the International Centre for the Settlement of Investment Disputes [ICSID]. These five organizations work together and separately to help finance developing countries in an effort to reduce poverty around the world. At this Web site you can access about a dozen World Bank periodicals including : (1) *World Bank News,* a weekly publication highlighting events, activities, and initiatives involving the World Bank (2) *Transition,* "A newsletter analyzing economic and social developments in transition countries, and reporting on related research, books, working papers, conferences, and articles" (3) *Development Briefs,* background information aimed at the media, business, academic, and government policy communities about the Bank's research, activities, and policies; and (4) *Poverty Lines*, "a brief, two-page newsletter which summarizes research on poverty."

World Neighbors Home Page
http://www.wn.org/index.asp

The U.S. based non-profit organization, World Neighbors seeks to eliminate hunger, disease, and poverty in Asia, Latin America, and Africa. World Neighbors is guided by the belief that "local knowledge and community participation are vital ingredients to finding flexible, workable solutions." The Web site contains information on World Neighbors' projects, speeches explaining the World Neighbors' empowering philosophy, articles about World Neighbors, and places and people connected to this organization. World Neighbors web site also lists links to Internet resources on international development.

E-Mail Directories of Anthropologists

WEDA—the Worldwide E-Mail Directory of Anthropologists
http://wings.buffalo.edu/academic/department/anthropology/weda/

Hosted by University of Buffalo's Anthropology Department, this is the site of WEDA, a searchable Worldwide E-Mail Directory of Anthropologists. WEDA is a volunteer project established to support communication between anthropologists (in the broadest sense of the word) around the world. Presently, this WEDA database contains addresses of more than one thousand institutions and more than three thousand individuals.

Embassies

List of Embassies in Washington, D.C.
http://www.cybertech-mall.com/embassy.html

This site offers a list of foreign embassies from A to Z located in Washington, D.C. This list includes the embassy address, telephone or fax number, and the national holiday for each country. This site may be useful for those about to travel abroad and who need information about the countries they plan to visit.

Environmental Anthropology

Alternatives Journal Home Page
http://www.fes.uwaterloo.ca/Research/Alternatives/alts.htm

Alternatives is the official journal of the Environmental Studies Association of Canada. It "aims to promote understanding and dialogue among scholars, professionals, activists, and students concerned about the environment, including its social and political dimensions." This Web site gives titles and abstracts for articles contained in current and recent issues. For example, the October-November 1995 issue includes the abstract for the article "A Rare Good Thing: The Hopi Solar Project and Barriers to the Use of Renewable Energy Technologies" by Dennis Bartels that focuses on the case of the Hopi Solar Project to show how economic factors impede the development of solar energy projects. The January-February 1996 issue contains the abstract for the article "Tracing the Trail of Tomasita the Tomato: Popular Education around Globalization" by Deborah Barndt that tracks the journey of a tomato from a Mexican plantation to a Toronto fast food restaurant in order to vividly illustrate the meaning of a global economy.

Alternative Technology Association Web Page
http://suburbia.net/~ata/

The Australian-based Alternative Technology Association aims to promote environmentally friendly technology. The Association publishes *ReNew*, a quarterly magazine of practical information about environmentally friendly technologies and about ways to incorporate those technologies into daily life. Topics covered include "The Toilet and the Environment," "Steam Powered House," and "Earth Covered Housing." There is also information related to alternative technologies, sustainable development, and renewable energy sources.

Anthropology & Environment Section of the American Anthropological Association
http://dizzy.library.arizona.edu/ej/jpe/anthenv/

The Anthropology and Environment Section aims to "foster research and communication issues relating to the interface between culture and the environment." The goal of this section is to provide an overview of the subspecialty of environmental anthropology.

Battelle Seattle Research Center
http://www.seattle.battelle.org/services/e&s/e&shome.htm#intro

Battelle Seattle Research Center is an organization that aims "to assist organizations and communities in managing their relationships with the environment and resolving conflicts in equitable and environmentally responsible ways." There is information on pollution prevention, and the Center posts the report "The Population-Environment Connection," an overview of the relationship between population size/composition and environmental change, with particular emphasis on the U.S. (rather than on Third World countries which tend to be the focus of attention).

Dam-Reservoir Impact & Information Archive: DRIIA
http://www.sandelman.ottawa.on.ca/dams/

The Dam-Reservoir Impact Information Archive is a joint project of the Canadian-based Dam-Reservoir Working Group and the Coalition to Preserve Hudson and James Bays. The Web site posts information on dams, water diversions, impoundments, hydroelectric projects, and on their impact around the world. You can find information on current and ongoing dam-reservoir disasters including the Auburn Dam (U.S.A.), Mekong Basin Projects (South East Asia), Three Gorges Project (China), and Yamdrock Tso Project (Tibet—built by China).

World Resources 1996-1997
http://www.wri.org/wri/wr-96-97/index.html

This World Resources Institute Web site offers access to hundreds of country-level and regional-level research on the condition of the environment and the state of natural resources. Reports are available for the following geographic regions and countries within each region: Africa, Asia, the Caribbean, Central America, Eastern Europe, Europe, New Independent States, North America, Oceania, South America, Commonwealth States, Latin America, and the Mediterranean.

Disaster Reports
http://www.vita.org/disaster/appeal/index.html

The U.S. Agency for International Development posts fact sheets describing the effects of disasters such as hurricanes, floods, civil wars, cyclones, and fires occurring in countries around the world.

E/The Environmental Magazine
http://www.emagazine.com/

E is an online magazine that publishes a variety of articles on environmental topics. The latest and archived issues are online. The March-April 1997 issue includes articles titled "The Roots of Recycling" which gives a brief historical overview of how people have dealt with garbage since ancient times (recycling and dumping); and "Jellyfish and Turtles" describing how Florida fishermen are benefiting from Chinese consumers' demand for jellyfish but not without adverse consequences to leatherback turtles who are dependent on jellyfish as a main food source.

Earth Negotiations Bulletin
gopher://gopher.igc.apc.org/11/pubs/enb

The *Earth Negotiations Bulletin*, published by the International Institute for Sustainable Development, is a comprehensive online reporting service of great value to those interested in international policy as it relates to "natural resource management, international environmental relations, sustainable development, and the issue of global governance." It offers up-to-date news on the United Nations, its policies, international conferences, and international negotiations on environment and development.

Earthwatch
http://gaia.earthwatch.org/

In the past 20 years, Earthwatch, a non-profit organization, has mobilized 1,845 projects in 109 countries. They expect 600 teachers and students to go on field expeditions in 1997. At this site, read about the new 1997 expeditions such as House of the Badlands, an archaeological exploration, and Mexican Art of Building, an artistic and architectural study of cultural and historic areas of Mexico. If this interests you, check out the expeditions catalogue for information on participation and membership (expedition costs range from $600 to $2,200, excluding airfare). Other exciting Earthwatch features include the college credit program, events calendar, employment opportunities, project results, and virtual field trips.

The EcoJustice Network
http://www.igc.apc.org/envjustice/

The EcoJustice Network "addresses environmental issues facing communities of color in the United States," including toxic hazards, environmental justice, and environmental racism. At this site, you can find out what interested parties are doing to combat environmental injustice on a local and global scale. For example, on the local level Communities for a Better Environment works to improve air and water quality in the San Francisco Bay Area and the Los Angeles Basin. On a global scale the Indigenous Environmental Network works to protect indigenous peoples from corporate policies or practices that damage their natural environment and otherwise pollute their territories. Check out "Immigration and the Rural Crisis in Mexico" by John Dury, and "Environmental Liberty and Social Justice for All: How Advocacy Planning Can Help Combat Environmental Racism" by Simmons Buntin.

Electronic Green Journal
http://www.lib.uidaho.edu/docs/egj.html

Electronic Green Journal, an online publication of the University of Idaho Library, publishes a variety of articles, bibliographies, reviews, and announcements for generalists and the specialists on environmental topics of global concern related to conservation, pollution, and development. At this site, articles and reviews from the most current as well as back issues can be accessed. Some examples of interesting titles include Ranjeev Benjamin's "Fish Mortality in Bengalore Lakes, India" and James R. Tobin's "The Wilderness Condition: Essays on Environment and Civilization."

EnviroLink
http://www.envirolink.org

EnviroLink claims to be "the largest online environmental information resource on the planet," connecting hundreds of environmental groups and organizations and millions of people from around the world and providing comprehensive and current online environmental information. The Envirolink Library can be accessed at this Web site along with Envirolink News Service, which posts "environmental news from news wire services throughout the world." Examples of news items include: "Uganda's Lakes Dying" and "Siberian Herders Squeezed by Oil and Gas."

Environmental Action Groups
http://earthsystems.org/civ.html

Environmental Action Groups is part of EcoWeb, a project of the Office of Recycling and Environmental Information at the University of Virginia in Charlottesville. EcoWeb facilitates access to recycling and other environmental information and resources. The list of links to Internet Web sites begins with AADCO (a vehicle disposal service) and ends with Zipperling (online environmental articles). Other examples of Internet resources include Association of Forest Service Employees for Environmental Ethics (AFSEE), Global Futures Foundation (GFF), and Earth Angels, an inner city children's group working to address environmental problems within their community.

Environmental Protection Agency
http://www.epa.gov/

The EPA's mission is to regulate and enforce laws regarding the use and disposal of solid wastes, pesticides, radioactive materials, and toxic substances. It also envisions a world in which individuals as well as institutions respect the environment and work together to protect and preserve it. The EPA allows you to choose a user category to find information resources geared to specific interests or perspectives. The categories are: (1) Kids (2) Students and Teachers (3) Researchers and Scientists (4) Business and Industry, and (5) State, Local, and Tribal Governments.

Environmental Protection Agency (EPA) Journal
gopher://gopher.epa.gov/11/.data/epajrnal

EPA Journal is published quarterly. The articles in each issue focus on environmental themes such as Earth Day or environmental awareness.

Global Stewardship Network
http://www.iisd.ca/linkages/gsn

This is a free news service covering issues related to global stewardship (that is, "caring for the earth and its current inhabitants, as well as a responsibility to leave to future generations a planet capable of sustaining life"). Past issues are also available at this site.

GreenClips
gopher://gopher.igc.apc.org/00/pubs/greenclips/66

GreenClips, an online news digest published by Chris Hammer of Sustainable Design Resources, summarizes programs and projects aimed at promoting environmentally safe and supportive building designs. This site offers an excellent overview of what is known as "green architecture." The summaries cover topics such as recycled materials, non-toxic products, and natural ventilation. It is updated every two weeks, and archived issues are available for reference at **http://solstice.crest.org/sustainable/greenclips/info.html** and **gopher://gopher.igc.apc.org/11/environment/pubs**

Greenpeace International Home Page
http://www.greenpeace.org

Greenpeace is an independent activist organization that confronts global environmental problems through nonviolent action "to ensure the ability of earth to nurture life in all its diversity." Greenpeace devotes specific "pages" to environmental problems: "Toxic Pages," "Nuclear Pages," "Atmosphere Pages," "Biodiversity Pages," and "Marine Pages." Check out "Hot Pages" to find out about high-priority environment campaigns.

Journal of Political Ecology Home Page
http://www.library.arizona.edu/ej/jpe/jpeweb.html

The Political Ecology Society (PESO) sponsors the *Journal of Political Ecology* (JPE), an electronic peer-reviewed journal that publishes articles and reviews in English, French, and Spanish. The journal publishes articles that focus on the relationship between the political economy and the human environment. Two issues of the journal are available online. Anthropology students might find Josiah McHeyman's "The Mexico-United States Border in Anthropology" useful because it critiques the two main approaches to studying the Mexico-United States' border society.

Native Americans and the Environment Web ite
http://conbio.rice.edu/nae/

The Center for Conservation Biology at University of California, Irvine, sponsors the Native American and the Environment Web site (be sure to choose "text only browser" if you are using one). For those new to this topic, see "Essay on Native American Environmental Issues" by David R. Lewis, which provides a brief overview of Native Americans' "sacred" relationship to their environment and the social and environmental issues they have confronted over time trying to maintain and manage it. Also, be sure to read "A Guide to Research on the Internet" by Alex Dark, which explains how to research Native North American environmental issues on the Internet. This guide also recommends other Internet resources
related to this topic. In addition to these two essays, this Web site includes bibliographies, a list of links to other relevant Web sites, and information about discussion groups.

New Urbanism
http://www.lawrence.edu/dept/anthropology/new_urbanism/NEW URBANISM.HTML

The "New Urbanism" page is the product of a joint effort between two students at Lawrence University: Kevin Kelly and Heather Tansey. New urbanism is a sustainable development movement "that puts people and the environment back into city designs." Kelly and Tansey provide background information on three city planners/developers and on four model cities: Celebration, Florida; Columbia, Maryland; Curetibe, Brazil; and Seaside, Florida.

Protecting Archaeological Sites Today (P.A.S.T.)
http:// home.uleth.ca/geo/jasweb/jasweb.htm

Protecting Archaeological Sites Today (P.A.S.T.) was created January 2, 1997, with the purpose of becoming a clearinghouse for information on "the preservation of archaeological, cultural, and historic sites, through political action and education." This organization seeks to preserve places threatened by corporate development, government actions, or other kinds of destructive behavior. There is a form to complete if you wish to list a site that is in such danger.

Rachel's Environment & Health Weekly
gopher://ftp.std.com/11/periodicals/rachel

The Environment Research Foundation sponsors the electronic edition of *Rachel's Environment & Health Weekly*, edited by Peter Montague. Each issue focuses on a health issue as it relates to the environment. Examples of issue topics include "Infectious Disease and Pollution," "The Pesticide Treadmill," "Fallout from the Peaceful Atom," and "Chemicals and the Brain."

Sierra Club Home Page
http://www.sierraclub.org/

Sierra Club is a San Francisco-based organization that supports the idea that "environmental rights are directly linked to human rights and that everyone has the right to a safe and healthy environment." Environmental conditions that endanger those rights are identified at this site in its two magazines, *Sierra* and *The Planet*, as well as its press releases and news briefs.

Sierra Club Policy: Archaeological Sites
http://www.sierraclub.org/policy/411.html

This site lists the Sierra Club's official policy on archaeological sites. It begins, "Archaeological resources are the material result of past human activity. These irreplaceable resources include, but are not limited to, artifacts, campsites, villages, dwellings, earth works, and rock art."

State of the World Indicators
http://www.igc.apc.org/millennium/inds/

This site provides links to various indicators for a quick overview of the state of the world's environment. Some indicators are water availability, species extinctions per day, and years until half of known crude oil is gone.

Sustainable Earth Electronic Library (SEEL)
http://www.envirolink.org/pubs/seel/about.html#brief

SEEL is a digital library sponsored by Sustainable Earth, a non-profit organization that uses the power of technology to promote environmental education. The mission of SEEL is to provide access to online publications from various environmental organizations and to promote communication and an ecological consciousness among participating organizations and individuals. The broad subject areas covered are: air and atmosphere environments, business and industry, hazardous waste, health and the environment, law, politics and government, plants and sustainable agriculture, society and environment, trees, forests and forestry, water, hydrosphere and aquatic environments, whole earth systems and conditions, and wildlife.

U.S. Water News Home Page
http://www.uswaternews.com/homepage.html

U.S. Water News Online posts national and international news related to water and water issues (water supply, quality, policy, legislation, conservation, rights, draughts and so on). News highlights successes as well as areas of concern. Examples of positive stories are "Southern California High Schools Help Promote Low-Flush Toilets," "Cleaner Water-Based Fuel Approved for Marketing" and "West Virginia Hosts Nation's Premier Water-Tasting Contest."

World Heritage Home Page
http://www.cr.nps.gov/worldheritage/

This is the World Heritage (U.S. branch) home page. World Heritage, a combined effort of the U.S. Department of the Interior, the National Park Service, and the U.S. Committee on the International Council on Monuments and Sites, identifies and protects cultural and natural sites in the United States threatened by development, neglect, or natural decay. This Web site includes guidelines for designating monuments, architectural works, and historical points, etc., as a "cultural heritage" or "national heritage." There is a list of 22 World Heritage sites in the United States that meet these guidelines and a tentative listing of properties under consideration.

World Resources Institute 1996-97 Press Release
http://www.wri.org/wri/press/wr96-nr.html

"The mission of the World Resources Institute (WRI) is to move human society to live in ways that protect the Earth's environment and its capacity to provide for the needs and aspirations of current and future generations." The news releases for 1996–1997 focus on environmental imbalances associated with urbanization.

Ethnography

American Ethnologist
http://www.ameranthassn.org/aespubs.htm

American Ethnologist is a quarterly journal produced by the American Ethnological Society, a division of the AAA. This site gives access to journal contents including abstracts. The journal publishes ethnographic research in the broadest sense of the term. Studying the abstracts and titles offers insights about the ethnographic approach to studying human groups and societies and may help you generate ideas for your own ethnographic research. For example the November 1996 issue (Volume 23, No. 4) includes papers on (1) a Corsican spelling contest as an effort to promote a minority language (2) the words and actions characteristic of the staff and residents at a shelter for the mentally ill and homeless, and (3) the process by which groups struggle to claim, define, and give meaning to culturally significant public spaces.

Culture of the Net (Research on)
http://www.vianet.net.au/~timn/thesis/index.html

This anthropology masters thesis by Tim North is an excellent example of ethnographic research. North argues that a new culture has emerged from the ever-growing population of Internet users and that the Internet has become a society with its own distinct culture. He describes that culture, emphasizing its impact on newcomers and the process by which they become enculturated. North presents more than the end product of his ethnographic research. He describes each step of the research process, explaining how he did his research. This is helpful for those doing their first research proposal or literature review, or those who need advice about how to gain entree, take notes, or write up research results.

Ethnographic Portraits (Of Arctic and Subarctic Peoples)
http://www.lib.uconn.edu/ArcticCircle/CulturalViability/portraits.html

These portraits include "An Introduction to Northern Peoples," "The Crees of Northern Quebec," "The Inupiat of Arctic Alaska," "The Nenets and Khanty of Yamal Peninsula, Northwest Siberia," "The Sami of Far Northern Europe," and "Greenland: a Modern Arctic Society."

Europe

Center for West European Studies
http://www3.pitt.edu/~wesnews/

The Center for West European Studies (CWES) is part of the University Center for International Studies. The Center, in conjunction with University Library system, sponsors the WWW Virtual Library: Western European Studies Home Page, with primary focus on identifying Internet resources related to Europe since 1945. In addition, the center publishes a monthly newsletter with current and past issues online. There is also an index of articles that have been featured in CWES newsletter.

Central European Online Home Page
http://www.centraleurope.com

At this Web site, get the headline news on Albania, the Czech Republic, Hungary, Poland, Romania, Russia, Slovak Republic, and Slovenia.

Europe
http://sunsite.berkeley.edu/

The Librarians' Index to the Internet includes the category "Europe." Select that category and find links to Web sites such as "Public Libraries—United Kingdom," "Bosnia Home Page," and "Central and Eastern European Languages."

Experts, Authorities, and Spokespersons

Yearbook of Experts, Authorities, and Spokespersons
http://www.yearbook.com/

The Broadcast Interview Source posts this Web site, which offers the addresses of experts, authorities, and spokespersons for various organizations. For information related to anthropological topics search by the appropriate keyword. For example, the word "refugees" produced six sources of possible information, each of which included an address, a profile, and a home page as applicable.

Fieldwork Photographs

Charles Lindholm
http://web.bu.edu/ANTHROP/faculty/lindholm/linphoto.html

Charles Lindholm, professor at Boston University, Department of
Anthropology, posts 10 photos of the Yusufzai Pukhtun of Swat in
Pakistan's mountainous Northwest Frontier Province.

Hunter Anthropology Fieldwork Gallery
http://maxweber.hunter.cuny.edu/anthro/field.html

The Hunter College (City University of New York) Department of
Anthropology posts photographs from faculty and student fieldwork.
Photographs are from fieldwork in Bulgaria, Tanzania, Turkey, Costa
Rica, Brazil, Spain, Syria, Israel, Nigeria, Iceland, Zaire, Mexico,
Namibia, Greece, Nebraska, Pennsylvania, and Florida. This site must
be viewed using Netscape.

Pacific Islands
http://www.cmp.ucr.edu/pacificislands/default.html

This Web site shows more than 50 photographs from Felicia R. and
E.R. Beardsley's ethnographic research in the Pacific Region. This site
must be viewed using Netscape.

Photographs of Mindanao, Philippines
http://www.xu.edu.ph/brandeis/gallery.html

Hans Brandeis, an ethnomusicologist from Berlin, posts photographs
from seven research trips to the Philippines. His "Gallery of
Photographs from Mindanao, Philippines" is of settlements, personal
adornment, rituals and ceremonies, and music and dance. Under the
music and dance section is an animated sequence of pictures depicting
a traditional priest playing a "boat" lute. This site must be viewed
using Netscape.

Photos from Faculty Fieldwork—Thomas Barfield
http://web.bu.edu/ANTHROP/faculty/barfield/barphoto.html

Thomas Barfield, professor and chair of the Department of
Anthropology at Boston University, posts slides and captions of two
groups of Nomadic people: the Central Asian Arabs of Afghanistan and
of the Kazgk Nomads of the Altari Mountains in Xinjiang, China.

Folklore

American Folklore Society
http://gopher.panam.edu:70/1gopher_root10%3a%5b000000%5d

The *American Folklore Society Newsletter* publishes interesting articles and information. Unfortunately the newsletters are long, and there is no table of contents, so you have to browse each one to see what they contain. However, if you have to do general research on folklore, the time you take to browse the newsletters will pay off with useful results.

Life History Manuscripts from the Folklore Project
http://lcweb2.loc.gov/wpaintro/wpahome.html

Life History Manuscripts from the Folklore Project was a product of the Works Progress Administration (WPA). The federal government established the WPA in the 1930s to give employment to those who could not find work during the Depression. Specifically, the WPA Federal Writers' Project (1936-1940) gave work to unemployed writers or to anyone who could qualify as a writer. Approximately 300 writers from 24 states interviewed people across the country from all walks of life and circumstances. The product of their efforts was a collection containing 2,900 documents ranging from 2,000 to 15,000 words. The collection can be searched by keywords (such as "textile workers," "immigrants," or "ex-slaves") and according to region or state.

Myths and Legends
http://pubpages.unh.edu/%7Ecbsiren/myth.html

Christopher Siren, a graduate student in physics at the University of New Hampshire, has created a virtual encyclopedia of links to Web sites on the WWW related to myths and legends. Siren organizes his links by cultural area (e.g., Greek and Roman, Slavic and Baltic, Native American, African). For example, the link to "African story lines" explains the Ashanti myth of "Anasi the Spider-man" and traces its path through African and Western mythology, and the link "Bigfoot legends" explores the legend of Bigfoot in Native American folklore.

Foreign-Language Dictionaries

Language
http://www.travlang.com/languages/

Do you need to talk to someone who speaks a foreign language? Identify the language(s) you speak and the one that you want to learn.

The computer will display common words and phrases such as "yes," "no," and "you're welcome" and words and phrases that will be useful when shopping, asking for directions, establishing a time and place to meet, and so on.

Online Dictionary Database
http://www.infovlad.net/linguistics/dic.html

This Web site contains an extensive list of links to foreign-language dictionaries. Simply indicate the language of interest and a list of links to Web sites posting the appropriate dictionary appears.

Foreign Newspapers

Library of Congress Foreign Newspapers
http://lcweb.loc.gov/global/ncp/oltitles.html#forn

On this site the newspapers are listed alphabetically. Papers range in title form *The Age* (Melbourne, Australia) to *Weekly Mail and Guardian* (Johannesburg, South Africa). Other countries with newspapers represented include Canada, Ecuador, India, Italy, Mexico, Nepal, Russia, and Sweden. Some of the newspapers are in English.

Newspaper Listing—Worldwide
http://www.dds.nl/~kidon/papers.html

This site provides links to a long list of foreign newspapers. Most of the newspapers are in their respective languages, but some are in English.

Forensic Anthropology

So You Want to Be a Forensic Anthropologist
http://taylor.anthro.umt.edu/studguid/forensic.htm

Randy Skelton, associate professor of anthropology at the University of Montana, Missoula, offers information and a number of valuable suggestions to those contemplating a career in forensic anthropology. Among other things Skelton covers job opportunities and graduate programs, and he recommends courses such as chemistry, biology, criminology, statistics, pharmacy, and psychology.

American Board of Forensic Anthropology (ABFA)
http://www.csuchico.edu/anth/ABFA/

The American Board of Forensic Anthropology was organized in 1977 to "provide, in the interest of the public and the advancement of the science, a program of certification in forensic anthropology." This Web site offers information regarding certification in forensic anthropology including a review of the application process and a list of certified forensic anthropologists (known as "diplomats") practicing in the United States.

American Academy of Forensic Sciences
http://www.aafs.org/weare.htm

"The American Academy of Forensic Sciences is a professional society dedicated to the application of science to the law." This site offers information about the annual meetings of the Academy, as well as information about how to become a member. Students who are currently enrolled in an "undergraduate, graduate, or accepted supervised training program leading to a career in one of the forensic science disciplines" are eligible for membership in the Academy.

RV's Forensic Anthropology Home Page
http://www.acs.appstate.edu/~rr13810/

R.V. Rickard, an anthropology student with a passion for forensic anthropology at Appalachian State University in North Carolina, offers some advice to students who share his interests. Also included are several papers Rickard wrote for forensic anthropology classes.

Gender

Demographic and Health Survey
http://www2.macroint.com/dhs/

The Demographic and Health Surveys (DHS) program, implemented by Macro International Inc. and funded primarily by the U.S. Agency for International Development (USAID), assists countries in "conducting national surveys on fertility, family planning, maternal and child health, and household living conditions" in order to obtain information on the "reproductive and health behavior of women throughout sub-Saharan Africa, the Near East, North Africa, Asia and Latin America." This Web site posts statistics on birth control methods, infant mortality rates, percentage of children immunized, and other reproductive health-related topics. DHS presents these statistics in the form of press releases. DHS also publishes a newsletter available online which includes articles on reproductive health. For example, the Vol. 7, No. 1 issue includes articles such as "Fertility and Family Planning in Egypt" and "Safe Motherhood in the Philippines." This site must be viewed through Netscape.

Dowry Deaths
http://rbhatnagar.ececs.uc.edu:8080/srh_home/1996_2/msg00193.html

This article by Partha Banerjee from Albany University examines the issues of bride burning and dowry deaths in India. *Dowry* is a payment of money or gifts given to a groom's family by the bride's family at the time of marriage. The author points out that there appears to be an increase in the number of brides murdered by the husband's family when the bride's family is unable to pay the full dowry. The author notes that dowry deaths are a "Hindu phenomenon" related to the caste system and a society unsupportive of unmarried women. This article includes a chart showing the geographical distribution of dowry deaths in India and the increase in the number of dowry deaths between 1987 and 1994. (The author acknowledges that the increase may also be attributed to increased coverage, which increases awareness of this issue.)

The Ethnic Woman International
http://www.thefuturesite.com/ethnic/eth-tble.html

The Ethnic Woman International is a journal established to "represent all women in a global society." It also serves as a forum by which those interested in women's issues can reach each other through "a combination of print and electronics." The current issue is online and the table of contents is posted for past issues.

FGM Research Home Page
http://www.hollyfeld.org/fgm

This site is supported by a handful of volunteers who offer little information about themselves or the organization they have formed. It posts a wide variety of information pertaining to the subject of female genital mutilation and includes information about how to join the e-mail discussion group, FGM-L, as well as archives of past listings from this group. For those of you who are interested in writing papers about this topic, this site offers a list of population groups around the world that practice FGM and information about U.S. policy on FGM. Also included is a list of advocacy groups around the world (and e-mail addresses), such as UNICEF, NOCIRC (National Organization of Circumcision Information Resource Centers), Si-Kata, and Forward that are dedicated to ending this practice.

Journal of South Asian Women's Studies
http://www1.shore.net/~india/bin/mfs/01/jsaws/index.htm

The online *Journal of South Asian Women's Studies* publishes a broad range of articles that address theoretical and practical issues of interest to both scholars of South Asia and to women living in or from South Asia (India, Nepal, Tibet, Afghanistan, Pakistan, Sri Lanka, Bangladesh, Bhutan, Burma, Thailand, Laos, Vietnam, Cambodia, Taiwan, Maldives, Malaysia, Indonesia, Philippines). Topics covered include law, civil rights, gender issues, religion, philosophy, politics, feminism and ecofeminism, classical and modern literature, poetry, dance, music, drama, language, translations, history, folklore, customs, medicine, architecture, and discoveries and cultural or social products by women.

Legislation Addressing FGM in the United States and Abroad
http://www.hollyfeld.org/fgm/legisl/index.html
    and
Female Circumcision Legislation
http://www.eskimo.com/%7egburlin/female.html

Interested in writing a research paper or learning more about the practice of female genital mutilation in the U.S.? These sites give information regarding the current legislation pertaining to the practice of FGM in the United States. For example, the first site gives information about bills that have been proposed in four states, California, Colorado, South Carolina and Rhode Island. The second site is a bill, written by Congresswoman Patricia Schroeder proposing to outlaw the practice of FGM in the United States on the federal level, and includes potential legal descriptions of what actions constitute FGM.

Progress of Nations, 1996
http://www.unicef.org/pon96/contents.htm

UNICEF posts the report *Progress of Nations, 1996* which contains articles, statistics, charts, and commentary on (1) women's physical well-being (2) nutrition/malnutrition (3) health, with emphasis on immunizations (4) education of women (5) the Convention on the Rights of Children, and (6) children's well-being in the industrial world.

Society for the Scientific Study of Sexuality (SSSS) Web page
http://www.ssc.wisc.edu/ssss/

The Society for the Scientific Study of Sexuality (SSSS), founded in 1957, is an international organization "dedicated to the advancement of knowledge about sexuality" and to "promoting human welfare by reducing ignorance and prejudice about sexuality." The SSSS believes in the "importance of both the production of quality research and the clinical, educational, and social applications of research related to all aspects of sexuality." This site contains the Statement of Ethics adopted by the SSSS, which offers a good overview of the topics covered under the subject of sexuality.

Voices of Women Article Library
http://www.voiceofwomen.com/articles/articles.html

This site features articles of interest related to women's issues including relationships, culture, family and community, survival skills, health issues, feminist concerns, and conflicts in the workplace. Examples of titles include: "The State vs. Midwives: A Battle for Body and Soul," "American Feminism in the Mid-Life Crisis," and "Media and Society." Voices of Women appears to be supported by a "market-place of Women-Friendly Web sites," all of which can be accessed via links posted on the site.

What Is FGM?
http://www.hollyfeld.org/fgm

This article describes the types of FGM performed around the world and in the U.S., offers some estimates of the number of women at risk of FGM, and describes efforts being taken around the world to abolish this practice. For those who are interested in further information on this topic, there is a list of books, films, and U.S.-based organizations.

Women of the World: Formal Laws and Policies Affecting Their Reproductive Lives
http://www.echonyc.com/~jmkm/wotw/

The Center for Reproductive Law & Policy, Inc. (CRLP) holds that "the promotion of women's reproductive rights is a crucial step toward the development of societies in which women hold equal status to men." This site focuses attention on six national governments and their formal laws, policies, and practices related to contraception, sterilization, abortion, population, and family planning. The six governments covered are those of Brazil, China, India, Germany, Nigeria, and the United States.

Human Rights

AAAS Human Rights Resources on the Internet
http://shr.aaas.org/dhr.htm

The American Association for the Advancement of Science (AAAS) sponsors the Science and Human Rights Program which was founded on the "premise that, as a matter of scientific freedom and responsibility, scientific societies should encourage international respect for the human rights standards embodied in the United Nations Universal Declaration of Human Rights and other treaties." This site offers various online resources relevant to the topic of human rights including a searchable database of Human Rights Internet sites and a searchable index of online publications.

Amnesty International Home Page
http://www.oneworld.org/amnesty/index.html

Amnesty International is devoted to the cause of human rights. The group focuses on prisoners of conscience, abuse by opposition groups, asylum seekers, and those in exile. It claims to be the world's largest international volunteer organization dealing with human rights with at least 1.1 million members in 150 countries and territories. Amnesty International posts their latest press releases, *Amnesty Journal*, and *Amnesty Reports*. This Web site also includes information useful to those seeking to address human rights abuses. In particular, see the links "Write a Letter, Save a Life," "Letter Writing Guide," and "Urgent Action Network."

Amnesty International Press Page—Archive
http://www.oneworld.org/amnesty/ai_press_archive.html#theme

If you need information on the general topic of human rights or a specific issue of human rights violations, this site serves as an excellent source. You can access reports covering news on Africa, the Americas, Asia, Europe, and the Middle East as well as special cases of pressing interest to Amnesty International.

Carter Center
http://www1.cc.emory.edu/CARTER_CENTER/

The Carter Center was founded by former President Jimmy Carter and is dedicated to fighting disease, hunger, poverty, conflict, and oppression by working for development, urban revitalization, and global health.

CESCR—The UN Committee on Economic, Social and Cultural Rights
http://shr.aaas.org/ESCR.htm

The "International Covenant on Economic, Social, and Cultural Rights" is a UN-drafted document outlining the guidelines UN member countries must follow to ensure human rights. This site posts a full text of the covenant, as well as country reports in which the Committee evaluates the constitution of each UN member country in light of these guidelines, describes the positive elements supporting human rights, and highlights the difficulties and challenges associated with implementing the covenant in that country.

Charity Organizations
http://www.charity.org/

This site is maintained by the International Service Agencies (ISA) with the primary mission of helping "millions of people overseas and in the United States who suffer from hunger, poverty, and disease or from the ravages of war, oppression, and natural disasters." This site contains a list of the 54 member agencies of ISA. Select an agency and access the corresponding home page. Examples of charity organizations referenced include American Refugees Committee, AmeriCare, Doctors Without Borders, Near East Foundation, and World Relief Corporation.

Human Rights and Related Sources Available through the Internet
http://www.umn.edu/humanrts/links/links.htm

The University of Minnesota Human Rights Library has compiled a list of links related to human rights. There are links to "International Law Documents," "Refugee and Aid Agencies," "International Criminal Tribunals," "Human Rights and International Law Electronic Publications," and "Internet Rights."

UNESCO Web Home page
http://www.unesco.org/

This is the home page of the United Nations Education, Scientific, and Cultural Organization (UNESCO). It currently consists of 185 member states, and its main objective is "to contribute to peace and security in the world by promoting collaboration among nations through education, science, culture, and communication in order to further universal respect for justice, for the rule of law, and for the human rights and fundamental freedoms which are affirmed for the peoples of the world." There are links to UN publications, press releases, speeches, and to documents describing international events and issues.

UNICEF Home Page
http://www.unicef.org/

The United Nations Children's Fund, founded in 1946, "is mandated by the United Nations General Assembly to advocate for the protection of children's rights, to help meet their basic needs, and to expand their opportunities to reach their full potential." *The State of the World's Children, 1997* report is available at this Web site along with background on the most widely ratified human rights treaty in the world known as *The Convention on the Rights of the Children.* There is also information on child labor. If you are looking for information on children's rights this is the place to start your research.

UN Indigenous Populations Documents
http://www.halcyon.com/FWDP/un.html

The Fourth World Documentation Project includes in its archives all UN documents, working papers and reports related to indigenous peoples. Some examples include the "Latest Draft Declaration on the Rights of Indigenous Populations," "The Uranium Industry and Indigenous People of North America," and "Self-Determination—The Australian Position."

Universal Declaration of Human Rights
http://www.amnesty.org/aboutai/udhr.htm

The Universal Declaration of Human Rights was "adopted and proclaimed by General Assembly Resolution 217 A (III) of 10 December 1948." This site offers the full text of this declaration, which is put forth "as a common standard of achievement for all peoples and all nations."

Indigenous Peoples

Aboriginal Studies
http://www.ciolek.com/WWWVL-Aboriginal.html

The Australian National University in conjunction with the Center for
World Indigenous Studies (CWIS) maintains the Indigenous Studies
WWW Virtual Library. There are links to 89 specialist information
facilities related to Australian Aboriginal Studies.

Bureau of Indian Affairs
http://www.doi.gov/bia/

The U.S. Department of Interior, Bureau of Indian Affairs, is
"responsible for the administration of federal programs for federally
recognized Indian tribes, and for promoting Indian self-determination."
The link "American Indian Heritage Day," gives access to the full text
of the proclamation by President Clinton declaring the month of
November "National American Indian Heritage Month." There are
links to other documents that chronicle the effort to set aside special
days, weeks, and months of the year to honor Native Americans. There
is also information on the meaning of Indian ancestry and information
on how to do genealogical research. BIA press releases cover court
decisions that affect Native American communities.

Columbus and the Age of Discovery Database
http://www.millersv.edu/~columbus/

The History Department and Academic Computing Services at
Millersville University have collaborated to create a Web site with
links to more than 1,000 sites related to the theme Columbus and the
Age of Discovery. Most of the articles piece together the past through
archaeological, anthropological, ethnographical, and historical research.
Some examples are: "Archaeological Artifacts from 'The Contact
Years'"; "Health and Diseases in the New World"; "How Columbus
Changed the World"; "Exchange of Plants and Animals between Native
Americans and Columbus"; "The Maroons of Jamaica"; and "Old
Foods in the New World." In one article, Mark Beach, staff writer of
the *Sunday News* asks a question that many anthropologists ask, "Did
Christopher Columbus, the Admiral of the Ocean Sea, discover
America in 1492, ushering in an "age of discovery"? Or, was it the
Arawak people of the Caribbean Islands who, discovering a somewhat
befuddled and disoriented Columbus, inadvertently [beckoned] the

beginning of the end for the continent's Indian cultures, bringing instead an "age of conquest"?

Fourth World Documentation Project Home Page
http://www.halcyon.com/FWDP/fwdptxt.html

This site is dedicated to covering the nations of the Fourth World—those "nations forcefully incorporated into states, which maintain a distinct political culture but are internationally unrecognized." It is estimated that there are 5,000 to 6,000 such nations. It is also estimated that one-third of the world's population are descendants of those who maintain distinct political cultures within governments that claim and govern their territories. Documents are catalogued according to the following categories: (1) African (2) European (3) Asian (4) Melanesian (5) Polynesian (6) Micronesian (7) North America (8) South American (9) Central America (10) Internationally Focused Documents (11) Tribal and Inter-Tribal Resolutions and Papers (12) United Nations Documents, and (13) Treaties, Agreements, and Other Constructive Arrangements. Examples of manuscripts online include "The Systematic Depopulation of Southern Sudan," "Nationalities Policies of the Soviet Union and China," and "Acknowledging the Illegal Annexation of Hawaii and Offering an Apology to Native Hawaiians."

Indigenous Studies
http://www.halcyon.com/FWDP/wwwvl/indig-vl.html

This WWW Virtual Library site is maintained by the Center for World Indigenous Studies (CWIS) "in conjunction with the Australian National University's Aboriginal Studies WW Virtual Library." CWIS holds that "access to knowledge and peoples' ideas reduces the possibility of conflict and increases the possibility of cooperation between peoples on the basis of mutual consent." This Web site offers links to Web pages related to "General Indigenous Studies Resources," and to Indigenous Studies Resources for Africa, Asia and the Middle East, Central & South America, Europe and the Pacific.

Institute of Indigenous Government
http://www.indigenous.bc.ca/rcap/rcapeng.html

"The Institute of Indigenous Government has created an online archive of the Final Report of the Royal Commission on Aboriginal Peoples." The Report consists of 5 volumes: (1) *Looking Forward, Looking Back* (2) *Restructuring the Relationship* (3) *Gathering Strength*

(4) *Perspectives and Realities*, and (5) *Renewal: A Twenty-Year Commitment.*

List of Federally Recognized Tribes
http://www.afn.org/~native/tribesl.htm

The Native American Information Resource Server posts a list of federally recognized tribes.

NAGPRA Documentation by Category
http://www.cast.uark.edu/other/nps/nagpra/

The Center for Advanced Spatial Technologies (CAST) at the University of Arkansas has placed on the Internet documents related to the Native American Graves Protection and Repatriation Act. The documents are sorted according to four categories: "Legal Mandates," "Guidance," "Notices," and "Review Committee." Full text of all documents is available online.

NAGPRA GUIDANCE: List of Tribal, Native Alaskan Entity, and Native Hawaiian
http://www.cast.uark.edu/other/nps/nagpra/nagpra.dat/gid003.html

This site outlines the Native American Graves Protection and Repatriation Act (NAGPRA) signed by President Bush in 1990. "The statute requires Federal agencies and museums that receive Federal funds to consult with Indian tribes, Native Alaskan entities, and Native Hawaiian organizations regarding the proper care and disposition of Native American human remains, funerary objects, sacred objects, and objects of cultural patrimony."

Native Americans and the Environment Web Site
http://conbio.rice.edu/nae/

The Center for Conservation Biology at University of California, Irvine sponsors the Native American and the Environment Web site. (Be sure to choose "text only browser" if you are using one). Particularly for those new to this topic, see "Essay on Native American Environmental Issues" by David R. Lewis which provides a brief overview of Native Americans' "sacred" relationship to their environment and the social and environmental issues they have confronted over time trying to maintain and manage it . Also, be sure to read "A Guide to Research on the Internet" by Alex Dark, which explains how to research Native North American environmental issues on the Internet. This guide also recommends other Internet resources related to this topic. In addition to these two essays, this Web site includes bibliographies, a list of links to other relevant Web sites, and information about discussion groups.

Native American Home Pages
http://www.pitt.edu/~lmitten/indians

This site is maintained by Lisa Mitten, a librarian at the University of Pittsburgh, who self-identifies as a "mixed blood Mohawk urban Indian." The goal of this Web site is "to provide access to home pages of individual Native Americans and Nations, and to other sites that provide solid information about American Indians." This page is organized according to the following categories: Information on Individual Native Nations; Native Organizations and Urban Indian Center; Tribal Colleges; Native Studies Programs and Indian Education; Native Media—Organizations, Journals and Newspapers, Radio and Television; Powwows and Festivals, and Sources for Indian Music; Native Arts Organizations and Individuals—Artists, Performers, Celebrities, Actors, Actresses, Singers, Musicians, Drum Groups, Storytellers, Authors, Activists; Native Businesses; General Indian-Oriented Home Pages.

Nativetech
http://www.lib.uconn.edu/NativeTech/

This Web site, maintained by the University of Connecticut, focuses on the technological aspects of Native American culture with an emphasis on the Eastern Woodlands region. The primary goal of this site is to disconnect "the term 'primitive' from peoples' perceptions of Native American technology and art." "The Web site is organized into categories of Beadwork, Birds & Feathers, Clay & Pottery, Leather & Clothes, Metalwork, Plants & Trees, Porcupine Quills, Stonework & Tools, and Weaving & Cordage." These categories also give information about how these materials are used by Native Americans and the history and background of these types of technologies.

Native Web
http://www.nativeweb.org/

Native Web is posted by the Global Affairs Institute of the Maxwell School and provides links to information about people from around the world who are classified as "native" by virtue of birth, by their governments, or by way of life. The purpose is "to provide a cyber place for the Earth's indigenous peoples" to communicate with one another and the world about "literature and art, legal and economic issues, land claims, and new ventures in self-determination."

Persons of Indian Ancestry
http://www.doi.gov/bia/ancestry/ancestry.html

This site describes how the government defines "Indian ancestry."

Top 25 American Indian Tribes for the United States
http://www.census.gov/ftp/pub/population/socdemo/race/indian/ailang1.txt

The racial statistics branch of the U.S. Census Bureau lists the top 25 American Indian tribes in the United States for 1980 and 1990. There is also a table that shows the percentage of change in membership for each tribe between 1980 and 1990.

UN Indigenous Populations Documents
http://www.halcyon.com/FWDP/un.html

The Fourth World Documentation Project includes in its archives all UN documents, working papers and reports related to indigenous peoples. Some examples include the "Latest Draft Declaration on the Rights of Indigenous Populations," "The Uranium Industry and Indigenous People of North America," and "Self-Determination—The Australian Position."

Journals Online

Alternatives Journal Home Page
http://www.fes.uwaterloo.ca/Research/Alternatives/alts.htm

Alternatives is the official journal of the Environmental Studies Association of Canada. It "aims to promote understanding and dialogue among scholars, professionals, activists, and students concerned about the environment, including its social and political dimensions." This Web site gives titles and abstracts for articles contained in current and recent issues. For example, the October-November 1995 issue includes the abstract for the article "A Rare Good Thing: The Hopi Solar Project and Barriers to the Use of Renewable Energy Technologies" by Dennis Bartels that focuses on the case of the Hopi Solar Project to show how economic factors impede the development of solar energy projects. The January-February 1996 issue contains the abstract for the article "Tracing the Trail of Tomasita the Tomato: Popular Education around Globalization" by Deborah Barndt that tracks the journey of a tomato from a Mexican plantation to a Toronto fast food restaurant in order to vividly illustrate the meaning of a global economy.

American Anthropological Association Journals and Newsletters

The following is a list of the 24 AAA-sponsored Journals and Newsletter. To access them directly, use the URL: **http://www.ameranthassn.org/** followed by the appropriate URL ending.

	URL ending
American Ethnologist	**aespubs.htm**
Transforming Anthropology	**abapubs.htm**
Voices	**afapubs.htm**
Occasional Paper of the Association of Senior Anthropologists	**asapubs.htm**
PoLAR	**aplapubs.htm**
The CommuNicAtor	**cnapubs.htm**
CSAS Bulletin	**csaspubs.htm**
Anthropology & Education Quarterly	**caepubs.htm**
General Anthropology	**cgapubs.htm**
Museum Anthropology	**cmapubs.htm**
Culture and Agriculture	**cagpubs.htm**
NASA Bulletin	**nasapubs.htm**
Teaching Anthropology/SACC Notes	**saccpubs.htm**
Anthropology of Consciousness	**sacpubs.htm**
SAE Bulletin	**saepubs.htm**
Anthropology of Work Review	**sawpubs.htm**
Cultural Anthropology	**~cultanth.htm**
Anthropology and Humanism	**shapubs.htm**
North American Dialogue	**sanapubs.htm**
Journal of Latin American Anthropology	**slaapubs.htm**
Journal of Linguistic Anthropology	**slapubs.htm**
Medical Anthropology Quarterly	**smapubs.htm**
Ethos	**ethos.htm**
City & Society	**suapubs.htm**
Visual Anthropology Review	**svapubs.htm**

American Journal of Archaeology
http://classics.lsa.umich.edu/AJA.html

This is the Web site of the official journal of the Archaeological Institute of America (AJA). It contains titles (no abstracts) for forthcoming, most recent, and past issues of the journal.

Archaeology Magazine
http://www.he.net/~archaeol/

Archaeology Magazine, the official journal of the Archaeological Institute of America, is one the oldest and most widely circulated scholarly journals of archaeology. The Web site posts news briefs, abstracts, some full-text articles, and a listing of events and museum shows related to archaeology. This is a good resource for persons new to the field of archaeology.

Academic Press Journal Sites
http://www.apnet.com/www/journal/

Academic Press has compiled a list of its academic journals with Web sites on the Internet. The list is presented alphabetically and according to subject. Academic Press publishes seven journal related to anthropology: *The International Journal of Nautical Anthropology, The Journal of Anthropological Archaeology, The Journal of Archaeological Science, The Journal of Historical Geography, The Journal of Human Evolution, Molecular Phylogenetics and Evolution,* and *Quaternary Research.* Abstracts of journal articles in every issue are available.

Cultural Anthropology Methods (CAM)
http://www.lawrence.edu/~bradleyc/cam.html

The journal *Cultural Anthropology Methods* publishes articles related to qualitative and quantitative methods in anthropology. The table of contents for all issues of CAM published since 1989 are online. The texts of three articles are online. One is on ethnographic sampling, a second is about cross-cultural research, and a third is a Guttman scale analysis of Matsigenka Men's Manufacturing Skills.

Cultural Studies and Critical Theory
http://eng.hss.cmu.edu/theory/

Cultural Studies and Critical Theory is a multidisciplinary journal that publishes research about contemporary texts and cultural practices. It welcomes submissions from those in a broad range of disciplines including anthropology, sociology, gender studies, feminism, literary criticism, history, and psychoanalysis. As a way of introducing readers to the field of cultural studies and critical theory, there are dozens of manuscripts online including the following titles: "Alien Abductions and the End of White People," "The Allure of Ethnic Eateries," "TV Heroines & Money Anonymous," "Writing, Knowledge and

Postmodern Anthropology," and "The World of The World of Coca-Cola."

Current Archaeology
http://www.compulink.co.uk/~archaeology/

This is the home page of Britain's leading archaeological magazine, *Current Archaeology*. At this site there is an index of articles published in *Current Archaeology*. The "Highlights" link allows access to selected major articles published in *Current Archaeology* that give readers an "introduction to some of the recent spectacular discoveries in British Archaeology." Examples of articles online include "Canterbury Cathedral—Were the Normans Better Builders than the Anglo-Saxons?" and "Feet!—Is It Possible to Distinguish between Celtic and Anglo-Saxon Skeletons From Their Feet?"

Electronic Green Journal
http://www.lib.uidaho.edu/docs/egj.html

Electronic Green Journal, an online publication of the University of Idaho Library, publishes a variety of articles, bibliographies, reviews, and announcements for generalists and the specialists on environmental topics of global concern related to conservation, pollution, and development. At this site, articles and reviews from the most current as well as back issues can be accessed. Some examples of interesting titles include Ranjeev Benjamin's "Fish Mortality in Bengalore Lakes, India" and James R. Tobin's "The Wilderness Condition: Essays on Environment and Civilization."

The Ethnic Woman International
http://www.thefuturesite.com/ethnic/eth-tble.html

The Ethnic Woman International is a journal established to "represent all women in a global society." It also services as a forum by which those interested in women's issues can reach each other through "a combination of print and electronics." The current issue is online and the table of contents is posted for past issues.

Getting Started in Oral Tradition Research—A Manual
http://tailpipe.learnnet.nt.ca/pwnhc/

The Prince of Wales Northern Heritage Centre supports the Gwich'in Social and Cultural Institute (GSC). The Institute documents Gwich'in oral history and traditional knowledge. A manual outlining the basic principles of oral tradition research has been posted. The manual defines oral tradition, written tradition, and traditional knowledge. It also gives advice on preparing for interviews, interviewing, processing information, and reporting results.

Human Organization—Journal of the Society of Applied Anthropology
http://www.smu.edu/~anthrop/humanorg.html

Human Organization publishes manuscripts "dealing with all areas of applied social science." At this site you can access titles and abstracts of articles, current and forthcoming issues. If you have to write a paper on applied anthropology, browse this site for ideas.

Journal of Field Archaeology
http://jfa-www.bu.edu/

The Journal of Field Archaeology is "an international, refereed quarterly journal serving the interests of archaeologists, anthropologists, historians, scientists, and others concerned with the recovery and interpretation of archaeological data. Its scope is worldwide and is not confined to any particular time period." The journal publishes field reports, technical and methodological studies, review articles, occasional general essays, and brief preliminary reports describing fieldwork. The titles and abstracts of the most recent issue and past issues are available at the Web site.

Journal of Human Evolution
http://www.hbuk.co.uk/www/ideal/journals/hu.htm

"*The Journal of Human Evolution* concentrates on publishing the highest quality papers covering all aspects of human evolution. The central focus is aimed jointly at palaeoanthropological work, covering human and primate fossils, and at comparative studies of living species, including both morphological and molecular evidence." This site offers abstracts of past and current issues via IDEAL USA.

Journal of Linguistic Anthropology
http://www.ameranthassn.org/slapubs.htm

Journal of Linguistic Anthropology is the journal of the Society for Linguistic Anthropology (a section of the American Anthropological Association). Titles and abstracts of articles published in the most recent issue are available online.

Journal of Political Ecology Home Page
http://www.library.arizona.edu/ej/jpe/jpeweb.html

The Political Ecology Society (PESO) sponsors the *Journal of Political Ecology* (JPE), an electronic peer-reviewed journal that publishes articles and reviews in English, French, and Spanish. The journal publishes articles that focus on the relationship between the political economy and the human environment. Two issues of the journal are available online. Anthropology students might find Josiah McHeyman's "The Mexico-United States Border in Anthropology" useful because it critiques the two main approaches to studying the Mexico-United States' border society.

Journal of the Society for Cultural Anthropology
http://www.pitzer.edu/~cultanth/frmain.htm

Cultural Anthropology, the journal of the Society for Cultural Anthropology, "welcomes contributions of relevance to cultural studies broadly conceived." Contents (titles only) of the most recent issue and past issues are available.

Journal of South Asian Women's Studies
http://www1.shore.net/~india/bin/mfs/01/jsaws/index.htm

The online *Journal of South Asian Women's Studies* publishes a broad range of articles that address theoretical and practical issues of interest to both scholars of South Asia and to women living in and from South Asia (India, Nepal, Tibet, Afghanistan, Pakistan, Sri Lanka, Bangladesh, Bhutan, Burma, Thailand, Laos, Vietnam, Cambodia, Taiwan, Maldives, Malaysia, Indonesia, Philippines). Topics covered include law, civil rights, gender issues, religion, philosophy, politics, feminism and ecofeminism, classical and modern literature, poetry, dance, music, drama, language, translations, history, folklore, customs, medicine, architecture, discoveries, and cultural or social products by women.

Journal of World Anthropology
gopher://wings.buffalo.edu/11/academic/department/anthropology/ jwa

The Journal of World Anthropology is an "electronic journal dedicated to scholarship in all fields of anthropology, and publishes articles on academic research, matters of theory and methodology, and the education of the public, as well as book, software and film reviews."

The journal "is produced and published at the State University of New York at Buffalo and distributed periodically."

Language (Journal of the Linguistic Society of America)
http://semlab2.sbs.sunysb.edu/Language/language.html

The table of contents and abstracts of articles published in current and back issues of *Language* are available at this Web site.

Linguistics Journals
http://www.lsadc.org/journals.html

The Linguistic Society of America posts a list of approximately 100 journals that publish articles related to the topic of linguistics along with the names of the organizations (and links) that publish them.

Paper Abstracts From 1996 AAA Annual Meeting
http://lucy.ukc.ac.uk/Cultcog/aaa96.html#H6

The American Anthropological Association posts abstracts from papers presented at the 1996 meeting. The theme of that meeting ("Culture as Distributed Cognition") encourages participants to explore the ways in which cultural knowledge is learned. Examples of papers presented included "The Social Construction of Ethnicity," "Reification and Social Reality in Modern Governments" and "The Social Distribution of Social Knowledge." Some of these abstracts may be difficult to read, as they were written for a professional audience; however, browsing through the titles may help you identify a topic for your own research and give you a basic overview of the research interests of anthropologists.

Papers from the Institute of Archaeology
http://www.ucl.ac.uk/archaeology/pia/

"*Papers from the Institute of Archaeology* (PIA) was launched in 1990 by a group of research students at the Institute of Archaeology, University College London" with the goal of providing an "outlet for research at the graduate level." Selected back issues of this journal are available online, while others are available for purchase. Each online issue contains full text of articles, book review, and abstracts of archaeology dissertations. Of particular interest are "The Problems and Prospects of Cultural Evolution" (Issue 1) and "Mortuary practices among the Aztec in the light of ethnohistorical and archaeological sources" (Issue 4).

The Scientist
http://www.the-scientist.library.upenn.edu/

The Scientist is "a bi-weekly periodical containing news and commentary on topics in the life sciences." This journal "uniquely focuses on news, issues, and trends that directly impact the career and professional interests of researchers." This site offers both current and past issues online, with full text of articles. Examples of articles published include "The Pope Reflects on Revelation and Theories of Evolution," which outlines the Catholic Church's position on biological evolution, "Maximizing Professional Development of Women in Academic Medicine," and "Collaborative Efforts Under Way to Combat Malaria."

Kinship

Family History Library
http://www.genhomepage.com/LDS.html

"The Church of Jesus Christ of Latter-Day Saints (LDS church) runs the Family History Library (FHL) in Salt Lake City, Utah. The FHL has one of the most impressive collections of genealogical material in the world." This site gives access to the addresses and home pages of various Family History Centers throughout the U.S. In addition, the FHL offers access to online databases such as the Social Security Death Index, the U.S. Colonial Vital Index, and the American Marriage Record.

The Genealogy Home Page
http://www.genhomepage.com/full.html

Genealogy Roots Corner is the organization that sponsors The Genealogy Home Page. "The goal of Genealogy Roots Corner is to gather researchers together on one site" to share information that will help others searching for missing branches of the family tree and seeking to make family connections. This is an excellent comprehensive "library" of information on the Internet including (1) Genealogy Guides (2) Libraries (3) Maps, Geography, Deeds and Photography (4) Newsgroups and Mailing Lists (5) Genealogy Societies (6) World Wide Genealogy Resources, and much more. There are more than 1600 links to Internet resources.

Kinship Tutorial, Main Menu
http://www.umanitoba.ca/anthropology/tutor/kinmenu.html

This excellent kinship tutorial was prepared by Brian Schwimmer, Department of Anthropology, University of Manitoba. The link "Kinship Fundamentals" begins the tutorial. Other links include systems of descent, kinship terminology, marriage systems, and residence rules. Three ethnographic cases help to bring kinship concepts to life. Those cases are a Turkish peasant village, the Yanomano of the Amazon Forest, and ancient Hebrews.

USGenWeb Project
http://www.usgenweb.com/

The USGenWeb Project is a non-profit organization with the goal of making "genealogical research material available through the Internet, ranging from various biographies to county vital records (birth, death, marriage), etc." Links to Internet sites are categorized according to the following levels: world, United States, and individual states. At the state level there are links to Web sites that give access to vital records, surname searches and links to other genealogical resources.

WorldGenWeb
http://www.dsenter.com/worldgenweb/index.html

The WorldGenWeb Project is maintained in conjunction with the USGenWeb Project, a non-profit organization with the goal of making "genealogical research material available through the Internet, ranging from various biographies to county vital records (birth, death, marriage), etc." This site offers links to Web pages offering genealogical information based in countries ranging from Afghanistan to Zimbabwe.

Latin America

Borderlines
http://lib.nmsu.edu/subject/bord/bordline

Borderlines is a monthly publication of the U.S./Mexico Project at the Interhemispheric Resource Center, an Albuquerque-based non-profit private research and policy institute. This online journal focuses on issues related to the ever-changing relationship between the United States and Mexico. Examples of articles include "Free Trade, Drug Trade" (explores the link between free trade and drug trade along the border), "Cross-Border Links and the Rise of Citizen Diplomacy" (examines the rise of border networks and coalitions), "Workers Succeed in Cross-Border Bid for Justice" (covers the story of *maquila* workers who won a sexual harassment suit filed against a U.S. employer), and "Cross-Border Indigenous Nation: A History" (describes the history of four Native American peoples separated by the border).

Latin America
http://sunsite.berkeley.edu/

The Librarians' Index to the Internet includes the category "Latin America." Select that category and find links to Web sites such as "Cuba Internet Resources," "Latin America Government Documents Projects," and "Latin America Studies."

Latin American Studies—WWW Virtual Library
http://lanic.utexas.edu/las.html

The Institute for Latin American Studies at the University of Texas hosts the Latin American Studies WWW Virtual Library. The library includes a country index and a subject index (African Diaspora to Women) of links to Internet resources.

LatinoLink News
http://www.latinolink.com/

LatinoLink offers news, analysis, commentary, and photo essays that explore the joys and challenges of people who call the United States home but who have roots in the countries of the Spanish-speaking Americas. Many interesting documents focusing on the meaning of the border and border activity.

Society for Latin American Anthropology
http://www.ameranthassn.org/slaa.htm

Established in 1969, the Society for Latin American Anthropology (a section of the American Anthropological Association), provides "a forum for discussion of current research, scholarly trends and human rights concerns in Latin America." The society's *Journal of Latin American Anthropology* "publishes articles on anthropological research in Mexico, Central and South America as well as the Caribbean, and it publishes works on peoples who move within the hemisphere by crossing national and/or cultural borders." The abstracts of this journal are available online.

"The Guide" to Internet Resources for Latin America
http://lib.nmsu.edu/subject/bord/laguia

Molly Molloy, Latin American specialist and reference librarian at
New Mexico State University Library, has prepared this guide to
Internet resources for Latin America. Her work is more than a list of
links. She gives an overview of the WWW and hints about how to find
Latin American resource information on the Internet.

Linguistics

Dictionaries on the Internet
http://www.bucknell.edu/~rbeard/diction.html

This Web site is "linked to more than 330 dictionaries of over 100
different languages" from Afrikaans to Zulu. There is also a variety of
specialized multilingual dictionaries (e.g., *French-English-Finish
Dictionary of Nuclear Terms, English-French-German Dictionary of
Health Finance*), subject specific dictionaries (e.g., *Cambridge
Dictionary of Epidemiology, Dictionary of U.S. College Slang*) and
thesauri.

English as a Second Language Home Page
http://www.lang.uiuc.edu/r-li5/esl/

Whether you are someone who is learning English as a second
language, a native speaker who needs to brush up on vocabulary, or
someone who is interested in how the English language is presented to
foreign-language speakers, this site is beneficial. This site presents
links related to "Listening and Speaking," "Reading," and "Writing."
Your computer must have audio capabilities in order to access
"Listening and Speaking."

Ethnologue: Languages of the World
http://www.sil.org/ethnologue/

"*Ethnologue* is a catalogue of more than 6,700 languages spoken in 228
countries. The *Ethnologue Name Index* lists over 39,000 language
names, dialect names, and alternate names. The *Ethnologue Language
Family Index* organizes languages according to language families." In
addition to the two indexes, the catalogue includes an introduction,
which gives an overview of language and its importance to human
interaction, and the issues linguistics study.

The Field of Linguistics
http://www.lsadc.org/flxtoc.html

The *Field of Linguistics* is posted by the Linguistic Society of America. It includes 22 essays explaining and clarifying the field of linguistics. Examples of essays include "Language Diversity," "Language and Brain," "Slips of the Tongue," "History of Linguistics," "Sociolinguistics," and "Endangered Languages."

The International Clearing House for Endangered Languages
http://www.tooyoo.L.u-tokyo.ac.jp/ichel.html

The International Clearing House for Endangered Languages is part of the Department of Asian and Pacific Linguistics Institute of Cross-Cultural Studies at the University of Tokyo. The *ICHEL Newsletter* includes summaries of papers presented at the International Symposium on Endangered Languages (November 18-20, 1995) including "The Scope of Language Endangerment and Recent Responses to It" by Michael Krauss, "Minority Language Policy and Endangered Languages in China and Southeast Asia" by David Bradley, and "On Language Maintenance and Language Shift in Minority Languages of Thailand: A Case Study of So (Thavung)" by Suwilai Premsrirat. See also the "The Endangered Languages Project: A Progress Report" and "UNESCO Red Book On Endangered Languages."

Journal of Linguistic Anthropology
http://www.ameranthassn.org/slapubs.htm

Journal of Linguistic Anthropology is the journal of the Society for Linguistic Anthropology (a section of the American Anthropological Association). Titles and abstracts of articles published in the most recent issue are available online.

Language
http://www.travlang.com/languages/

Do you need to talk to someone who speaks a foreign language? Identify the language(s) you speak and the one that you want to learn. The computer will display common words and phrases such as "yes," "no," and "you're welcome" and words and phrases that will be useful when shopping, asking for directions, establishing a time and place to meet, and so on.

Language (Journal of the Linguistic Society of America)
http://semlab2.sbs.sunysb.edu/Language/language.html

The table of contents and abstracts of articles published in current and back issues of *Language* are available at this Web site.

Language in Cross-Cultural Understanding
http://www.halcyon.com/fkroger/bike/language.htm

This essay by David Mozer emphasizes the importance of language for determining how we view the world. The author points out that biases are ingrained in our everyday language, and in order to accurately describe a culture, we must recognize and alleviate biases through careful use of our words. The author also provides some tips on how to become "more sensitive, objective, and accurate in (our) observations of non-western cultures."

Linguistic Society of America
http://www.lsadc.org/

The Linguistic Society of America, founded in 1924 and with a membership of 7,000, posts basic information about its organization along with the program of its annual meetings. Of particular interest to the linguistics student are the organization's statements and resolutions on issues such as "Language Rights," "Ebonics," "Research with Human Subjects," and "English Only Initiatives." The organization also posts of list of approximately 100 journals that publish articles related to linguistics. Finally, check out The *Field of Linguistics* a series of 22 essays explaining and clarifying the field of linguistics. Examples of essays include "Language Diversity," "Language and Brain," "Slips of the Tongue," "History of Linguistics," "Sociolinguistics," and "Endangered Languages."

Linguistics FAQ
http://www.lsa.umich.edu/ling/lingfaq.html

Linguistics at the University of Michigan's Program in Linguistics answer some frequently asked questions about the field of linguistics including 1) What is linguistics? 2) What do you mean by "human language"? 3) How old is linguistics? and 4) What can I do with a linguistics major?

Linguistics Journals
http://www.lsadc.org/journals.html

The Linguistic Society of America posts a list of approximately 100 journals that publish articles related to the topic of linguistics along with the names of the organizations (and links) that publish them.

Online Dictionaries
http://www.infovlad.net/linguistics/dic.html

This is an extensive list of foreign-language dictionaries, from Arabic vocabulary lists to a Welsh-to-German dictionary.

Online Dictionary Database
http://www.infovlad.com/linguistics/dic.html

This Web site contains an extensive list of links to foreign-language dictionaries. Simply indicate the language of interest and a list of links to Web sites posting the appropriate dictionary appears.

Society for Linguistic Anthropology
http://www.ameranthassn.org/sla.htm

The Society for Linguistic Anthropology was founded in 1983 "to advance the study of language in its social and cultural context and to encourage communication of the results of such study." The society's bylaws, publication, and the names, addresses, and phone/fax numbers of its officers can be accessed.

Translator's Home Companion
http://www.lai.com/lai/companion.html

The Translator's Home Companion is "intended to serve as a focal point of information about resources available on the Internet and elsewhere for translators, interpreters, and all those interested in the arts and crafts of foreign languages." There are links to "The Latest News of the Translation World," "Searchable Directories of Translators," "Translation Organizations," "Dictionary Reviews," "Online Dictionaries and Glossaries," and much more.

The World Wide Web Virtual Library: Linguistics
http://www.emich.edu/~linguist/www-vl.html

This is a library of links maintained by the University of Michigan's Program in Linguistics. The links are organized according to the following broad topics: 1) The Profession, 2) Research and Research Support, 3) Publications, 4) Pedagogy, 5) Language Resources, 6) Computer Support, and 7) New Resources.

Medical Anthropology

Association of American Indian Physicians
http://www.aaip.com/

Founded in 1971 by 13 Indian physicians as both a forum for those interested in the practice of Indian medicine and to serve the increasing number of Indian physicians, this site offers a wide variety of information concerning traditional medicinal practices within the American Indian culture. Of particular interest is the Centers for Disease Control (CDC) report *CDC's Diseases: Closing the Gap.* The report is particularly interesting in that it describes the CDC's current plans to establish surveillance strategies to identify and report new and emerging infectious diseases. This plan includes "traditional" health care providers as part of the worldwide surveillance team.

The Brunel M.A. in Medical Anthropology
http://http1.brunel.ac.uk:8080/~hssrsdn/courses/medanth.htm#s1

This document was prepared by Stuart Neilson at the Centre for the Study of Health, Sickness, and Disablement at Brunel, the University of West London. The author gives an overview of the field of medical anthropology and explains the value of the anthropological perspective to health professionals (i.e., radiology technicians, physical therapists, and nurses).

Centers for Disease Control and Prevention Home Page
http://www.cdc.gov/

The CDC administers national programs aimed at the prevention and control of diseases, injury, and other preventable conditions. It develops and enacts programs to deal with environmental health problems such as chemical and radiation emergencies. It is also responsible for collecting and making available to the public national data on health status and health services.

Dental Anthropology Association
http://www.sscf.ucsb.edu/~walker/index.html

The Dental Anthropology Association, maintained by the University of California at Santa Barbara, seeks to "stimulate interest in the field of dental anthropology and to promote the exchange of educational, scientific, and scholarly knowledge in the field." Browse the bibliography section for articles on dental topics published in the *American Journal of Physical Anthropology* between 1975 and 1996. The association also lists links to Web sites of interest to Dental Anthropologists.

Global Childnet
http://edie.cprost.sfu.ca/gcnet

Global Childnet, headquartered in Vancouver, seeks to provide access to credible information on child-related issues and to promote communication on a global scale about these issues. At this Web site you can access the most recent issue of *Global Child Health News and Review*, which includes news, opinion, and feature stories. Examples of the kinds of medical issues covered are reflected in the following titles: "Are We Paying Enough Attention to Mother's Health?" "The Mother-Baby Package: WHOs Guidelines Map the Road to Safer Motherhood," "Adolescents with HIV/AIDS," and "The Risks of Tobacco Use: A Message to Teens."

National Institutes of Health
http://www.nih.gov/

The National Institutes of Health (NIH) mission is "to uncover new knowledge that will lead to better health for everyone." As of March 24, 1997, the NIH database contained 49,085 documents on 159 NIH Internet services. In light of the large number of documents, perhaps the best way to approach this Web site is to use its search engine. Keywords relevant to those interested in medical anthropology include: alternative medicine, holistic medicine, culture, women's health, immigration, and special populations (Native Americans, Latin Americans, etc.).

Office of Minority Health Research Center
http://www.omhrc.gov/

The Office of Minority Health Resource Center serves as a point of contact to those seeking information on minority health. The "Publications" link gives access to the bimonthly newsletter *Closing the Gap*. Each issue addresses special health topics of concern to minority communities. The "Database" link leads to resources and publications on specific minority communities: African Americans, Asians, Hispanics/Latinos, Native Americans, Native Hawaiians, and Pacific Islanders.

PAHO—Country Health Profiles Information
http://www.paho.org/english/country.htm

The Pan American Health Organization assesses the health situation in each country that is part of the Americas. Available for each country are specific health problems (statistics and a brief overview), demographic characteristics (size, distribution, and age-specific population characteristics), and descriptions and statistics related to health services and resources.

U.S. Department of Health and Human Services
http://www.os.dhhs.gov/

The Department of Health and Human Services (DHHS) is a government agency charged with the tasks of protecting the health of all Americans and of providing basic services, especially to the most disadvantaged segments of the population. The DHHS encompasses more than 300 programs engaged in a wide range of activities (e.g. preventing outbreaks of infectious diseases, immunization, assisting low-income families, preventing child abuse). The News and Public Affairs link gives access to the news, speeches and press releases since 1991. Titles include "Disability Rate Among Older Americans Declines Dramatically," "The Tyranny of Thinness Obsession," and "Cancer Research in Brief."

U.S. National Library of Medicine
http://www.nlm.nih.gov/nlmhome.html

The National Library of Medicine (NLM) "provides a wide variety of resources related to biomedical and health science, both past and present." Some particularly interesting features include:
1) The newsletter *AIDS Treatment News*, beginning with the April 8, 1988 issue.
2) Online exhibitions of art, history and images connected with medicine.
3) Images from the history of medicine including nearly 60,000 prints, photographs, and artwork from the history of medicine division.
4) Visible human images link connects you to a sample of anatomic images of male and female humans.

World Health Organization Press Releases
http://www.who.ch/press/1996pres.htm

The World Health Organization acts as "the directing and coordinating authority on international health work." Submit a keyword such as "malaria" or "Zaire" to see a list of all the press releases related to that disease or to health-related issues in that country. You can also choose to scroll through the list of press releases.

Middle East

Middle East Peace Process
http://www.arts.mcgill.ca/MEPP/mepp.html

The Inter-University Consortium for Arab Studies was established in 1989, and is a "collaborative project of McGill University and the Université de Montréal, together with associated researchers based at other institutions." ICAS attempts to "promote and facilitate research on the contemporary Arab world (and the broader Middle East region) through its pursuit of four interrelated mandates: 1) the encouragement of academic cooperation and research collaboration among local scholars, and between researchers in Québec/Canada, the Middle East, and the rest of the world 2) the provision of research resources accessible to students and scholars 3) the pursuit of specific research projects, under the auspices of the Consortium, on the contemporary Arab world, and 4) support for the training and research of an emerging generation of scholars." This site offers links to a number of Internet-based ICAS-sponsored projects on the Middle East peace process including the Palestinian Refugee Research Net, Palestinian Development Info Net, and the Palestinian NGO Support Project.

Middle East Studies Association of North America (MESA)
http://www.mesa.arizona.edu/

MESA is a non-profit organization created in 1966 with the goal of "promoting high standards of scholarship and instruction, facilitating communication among scholars through annual meetings and publications, and promoting cooperation among those who study the Middle East." At this site you can find selected articles from the *MESA Bulletin*, a semi-annual publication, and information about MESA-affiliated organizations such as Association of Central Asian Studies (ACAS), Association of Israel Studies (AIS), and the Middle East Librarians Association (MELA). Depending on your research interests, you may want to check to see if any of these organizations have Web sites.

The Center for Middle Eastern Studies
http://menic.utexas.edu/menic

This site, sponsored by the University of Texas at Austin, provides a variety of resources for those people interested in the Middle East. Subject categories include "Ancient history/Archaeology," "Arts/Culture," "Business/Finance/Economics," and "Maps/Travel, and Regional Information." Also included in these subject categories are relevant links to over 20 countries in the Middle East including Saudi Arabia, Kuwait, and Afghanistan.

Middle East
http://kahn.interaccess.com/intelweb/mideast.html

This Web site is part of the Online Intelligence Project, which is "oriented to individuals and professionals with an interest in international news, commerce, and references." The Middle East section offers a wide variety of information on that region of the world. For example, the section on Israel and Palestine provides a link to the *Jerusalem Post*, to the U.S. State Department page on the Middle East Peace Process, and to information on the Palestinian economy and government. Other countries covered by the Online Intelligence Projects include India, Pakistan, Iran, and Afghanistan.

Middle East
http://sunsite.berkeley.edu/

The Librarians' Index to the Internet includes the category "Middle East." Select this category and find links to Web sites such as "Middle East Studies Resources," "Arab.net," and "Iranian Cultural and Information Center."

Middle East Studies Resources
http://www.columbia.edu/cu/libraries/indiv/area/MiddleEast/index.html

"Columbia University's collection of Middle East Studies Internet Resources is an on-going compilation of electronic bibliographic resources and research materials on the Middle East and North Africa" organized by region, by country, and by subject. Middle East resources by subject include "Foods of the Middle East," "Languages of the Middle East," "Minorities of the Middle East," "Political Violence of the Middle East," "Water in the Middle East," and "Electronic Journals and Newspapers in the Middle East."

Encyclopedia of the Orient
http://i-cias.com/e.o/index.htm

This site is an online encyclopedia devoted to topics related to countries in the Middle East. It includes information on each country's economy, history, politics, health, education, and religion. There is also information on life in and the history of the Middle East in general. Search by keyword to find specific information.

Multiracial People

Interace Database
http://www.compumedia.com/%7Emulato/InteraceDatabase.html

This site is a resource for those interested in the lives and treatment of mixed-race people. It lists links to articles, organizations, films, databases, journals, and other resources on the Internet.

Interracial Voice
http://www.webcom.com/%7Eintvoice/

Interracial Voice publishes articles that focus on the shortcomings of the U.S. racial classification system and that clarify the need for a new "racial" category for interracial individuals.

Museums

The Future of the Past
http://www.cc.ukans.edu/~hoopes/mw/

"The Future of the Past: Archaeology and Anthropology on the World Wide Web" is a paper written by John W. Hoopes of the Department of Anthropology and the Museum of Anthropology at the University of Kansas. In it Hoopes examines "ways that one can use the Web to enhance research and improve access to a variety of archaeological and ethnographic materials" held by museum collections.

International Council of Museums (ICOM) Web Page
http://ww.icom.org/

The International Council of Museums (ICOM), created in 1946 with 13,000 members in 145 countries, is "devoted to the promotion and development of museums and the museum profession at an international level." The site posts a chronology from 1946 to 1996 of information pertaining to ICOM events and happenings. The site also provides information on International Museum Day, created for museum professionals to promote museum awareness. Check out the "Virtual Library Museum Home Pages," which functions as a directory of museums that can be accessed via the Internet.

Peabody Museum of Archaeology and Ethnology
http://fas-www.harvard.edu/~peabody/

"Founded in 1866, the Peabody Museum is the oldest museum in this hemisphere devoted entirely to the disciplines of archaeology and ethnology." This site offers online exhibits including "Rainmakers from the Gods: Hopi Katsinam," "Against the Winds: American Indian Running Traditions," "Three Generations of Women," "Anthropologists," and "The Children of Changing Woman." This site is best viewed using Netscape.

The Smithsonian Institution Home Page
http://www.si.edu/start.htm

This site enables you to "explore information on the Smithsonian's many museums, galleries, research centers, and offices both in and outside the Washington, D.C. metropolitan area." There is also information on the history of the Smithsonian museums and on traveling exhibits. If you have Netscape, you can take a three-minute "virtual" tour of the Smithsonian. Check out the Smithsonian's information on fellowship and internship opportunities.

The University of Pennsylvania Museum of Archaeology and Anthropology
http://www.upenn.edu/museum/

The University of Pennsylvania's Museum of Archaeology and Anthropology offers online exhibitions such as "Living in Balance: the Hopi, Zuni, Navajo, and Apache," "Time and Rulers at Tikal: Architectural Sculpture of the Maya," "The Ancient Greek World," "Ancient Mesopotamia: The Royal Tombs of Ur," "The Egyptian Mummy: Secrets and Science," "Raven's Journey: Alaska's Native People," and "Buddhism: History and Diversity of a Great Tradition." Also included at this site are "galleries with material from China, ancient Egypt, Mesoamerica, North America (Plains Indians), Polynesia, and Africa."

We have included a small sample of the hundreds of museums with homepages on the Internet. They are listed according to seven categories (1) Africa (2) Asia (3) Folk Art (4) General Resources (5) Latin America (6) Native Americans, and (7) Natural and Cultural History.

African Museums

Brooklyn Museum
http://wwar.com/brooklyn_museum/index.html

California African-American Museum
http://www.caam.ca.gov/

Nok—The Museum of African Art @Harlemm
http://harlemm.com/nokbeta/

Peabody Essex Museum
http://www.pem.org/

Asian Museums

Asian Art Museum of San Francisco
http://www.asianart.org/

Brooklyn Museum
http://wwar.com/brooklyn_museum/index.html

China the Beautiful
http://www.ChinaPage.com/

Chinese-American Museum
http://members.aol.com/mcahla/cam.htm

Korean American Museum
http://home.lacn.org/lacn/kam/

Kyoto National Museum
http://www.kyohaku.go.jp/

National Museum of Ethnology
http://www.minpaku.ac.jp/

Oriental Institute Museum
http://www-oi.uchicago.edu/OI/MUS/OI_Museum.html

Peabody Essex Museum
http://www.pem.org/

Folk Art Museums

American Folk Art Museum
http://www.folkartmuse.org/toc.html

California African-American Museum
http://www.caam.ca.gov/

Museum of International Folk Art
http://www.state.nm.us/moifa/

General Resource Museums

Allentown Art Museum
http://www.regiononline.com/~atownart/

Anthropology and Archaeology Museums and Exhibits
http://www.ucmp.berkeley.edu/subway/anthro.html

American Folk Art Museum
http://www.folkartmuse.org/toc.html

Asian Art Museum of San Francisco
http://www.asianart.org/

Bishop Museum
http://www.bishop.hawaii.org/

Brooklyn Museum
http://wwar.com/brooklyn_museum/index.html

California African-American Museum
http://www.caam.ca.gov/

Carnegie Museum of Natural History
http://www.clpgh.org/cmnh/

China the Beautiful
http://www.ChinaPage.com/

Chinese-American Museum
http://members.aol.com/mcahla/cam.htm

Field Museum of Natural History
http://www.fmnh.org/Home.htm

Fowler Museum of Cultural History
http://www.fmch.ucla.edu/

French Ministry of Culture
http://www.culture.fr/

The Gold Museum
http://www.banrep.gov.co/museo/ingles/home.htm

Heard Museum
http://hanksville.phast.umass.edu/defs/independent/Heard/Heard.html

Illinois State Museum
http://www.museum.state.il.us/

Intuit: The Center for Intuitive and Outsider Art
http://outsider.art.org/

Israel Museum
http://www.imj.org.il/

Korean American Museum
http://home.lacn.org/lacn/kam/

Kyoto National Museum
http://www.kyohaku.go.jp/

McClung Museum
http://mcclungmuseum.utk.edu/

Mexican Museum
http://www.folkart.com/~latitude/museums/m_mexsf.htm

Milwaukee Public Museum
http://www.mpm.edu/

Morikami Museum and Japanese Gardens
http://www.folkart.com/~latitude/museums/m_mexsf.htm

Museum of International Folk Art
http://www.state.nm.us/moifa/

Museum of Natural History
http://oregon.uoregon.edu/~mnh/index.html

MuseumNet
http://www.museums.co.uk/

Museum of Victoria
http://www.mov.vic.gov.au/

Museo de las Culturas Prehispanicas
http://mexplaza.udg.mx/Museo/

Natural History Museum of Los Angeles County
http://www.lam.mus.ca.us/webmuseums/main.shtml

National Museum of Ethnology
http://www.minpaku.ac.jp/

Native American Heritage Museum State Historic Sites
http://history.cc.ukans.edu/heritage/kshs/places/nahm.htm

Oriental Institute Museum
http://www-oi.uchicago.edu/OI/MUS/OI_Museum.html

Peabody Essex Museum
http://www.pem.org/

Peabody Museum of Natural History
http://www.peabody.yale.edu/

Pecos Rio Grande Museum of Early Man
http://www.wenetco.com/pecosrio/

Pueblo Cultural Center
http://hanksville.phast.umass.edu/defs/independent/PCC/PCC.html

San Jose Art Museum
http://gallery.sjsu.edu/

Southwest Museum
http://www.annex.com/southwest/museum.htm

UC Museum of Paleontology
http://www.ucmp.berkeley.edu/museum/museum.html

Virtual Library Museums Page
http://nic.icom.org/vlmp/

WebMuseum, Paris
http://www.oir.ucf.edu/wm/

Latin American Museums

The Gold Museum
http://www.banrep.gov.co/museo/ingles/home.htm

Mexican Museum
http://www.folkart.com/~latitude/museums/m_mexsf.htm

Museo de las Culturas Prehispanicas
http://mexplaza.udg.mx/Museo/

Pecos Rio Grande Museum of Early Man
http://www.wenetco.com/pecosrio/

Native American Museums

Heard Museum
http://hanksville.phast.umass.edu/defs/independent/Heard/Heard.html

Native American Heritage Museum State Historic Sites
http://history.cc.ukans.edu/heritage/kshs/places/nahm.htm

Peabody Essex Museum
http://www.pem.org/

Pueblo Cultural Center
http://hanksville.phast.umass.edu/defs/independent/PCC/PCC.html

Southwest Museum
http://www.annex.com/southwest/museum.htm

Natural and Cultural History Museums

Bishop Museum
http://www.bishop.hawaii.org/

Carnegie Museum of Natural History
http://www.clpgh.org/cmnh/

Field Museum of Natural History
http://www.fmnh.org/Home.htm

Fowler Museum of Cultural History
http://www.fmch.ucla.edu/

Illinois State Museum
http://www.museum.state.il.us/

McClung Museum
http://mcclungmuseum.utk.edu/

Museum of Natural History
http://oregon.uoregon.edu/~mnh/index.html

Museum of Victoria
http://www.mov.vic.gov.au/

Peabody Essex Museum
http://www.pem.org/

Peabody Museum of Natural History
http://www.peabody.yale.edu/

Nacirema

Nacirema Web: Resources on the Nacirema People
http://www.beadsland.com/nacirema/

The Nacirema Web offers various resources that relate to the study of
the Nacirema people, including the famous work "Body Rituals among
the Nacirema." The goal of this Web site is to heighten
anthropologists' awareness of the importance of cultural relativity.

Although "Body Rituals among the Nacirema," is a humorous look at the anthropologist's tendency to describe events in foreign cultures from an ethnocentric point of view, the essay reminds us that it is important to remain non-judgmental when observing and describing other cultures.

North America

Association for Studies in Canadian-American Relations
http://www.tile.net/tile/listserv/ascarl.html

The Association for Studies in Canadian-American Relations "seeks to encourage and facilitate communication and information exchange among members of the academic and policy community who specialize in Canadian-American relations and Canadian policy towards the United States." There are links to Web sites related to foreign affairs, citizenship, immigration, trade environment, and natural resources.

Canadian Sociology and Anthropology Association
http://artsci-ccwin.concordia.ca/SocAnth/csaa/csaa_hm.html

The Canadian Sociology and Anthropology Association "promotes research, publication, and teaching in Anthropology and Sociology in Canada." The society publishes a journal, *The Canadian Review of Sociology and Anthropology*. Newsletters are published monthly and the two most recent issues are online. Of particular interest to students are the links to sociology and anthropology departments in Canada. The association also posts information on its annual conference, membership, and ethics.

Links to Canadian Cultural Sites
http://www.dfait-maeci.gc.ca/english/culture/sites.htm

The Canadian Department of Foreign Affairs and International Trade has compiled a list of links to significant cultural organizations and prospects in that country such as Canadian Broadcasting Corporation, Canadian Museum of Civilization, Aboriginal Art Gallery, and the National Film Board.

North America
http://sunsite.berkeley.edu/

The Librarians' Index to the Internet includes the category "North America." Select this category and find links such as "Index of Native

American Resources," "African American History," and "Culture and Society of Mexico."

North American Institute (NAMI)
http://www.santafe.edu/~naminet

The North American Institute (NAMI) "is a tri-national public affairs organization which studies the emerging regional space of Canada, U.S., and Mexico and the development of the North American communities" with special emphasis on trade, institutional developments, and social cultural roots of identity. The NAMINews is available online.

Statistics Canada
http://www.statcan.ca/

The Canadian government publishes a wide variety of information related to the 1996 census, land, people, economy, government, justice, and crime.

Pacific Islands

Center for Pacific Islands Studies
http://www2.hawaii.edu/shaps/pacific/

The Center for Pacific Islands Studies (CPIS) at the University of Hawaii at Manoa is "the only academic center in the United States that focuses solely on the islands of the Pacific." This Web site offers the current issue of the CPIS newsletter online, as well as links to Internet resources on the Pacific Islands and a guide to films about the Pacific.

South Pacific Centre for Communication Information and Development
http://pactok.net.au/docs/nius/spcencid.htm

The South Pacific Centre for Communication and Information in Development (SPCenCIID) of the University of Papua, New Guinea is devoted to the study of Third World or development journalism with emphasis on the South Pacific (American Samoa, Belau, Cook Islands, Fiji, Papua, New Guinea, Tahiti, Tonga, and Western Samoan). Of particular interest is the Centre's journal, *Pacific Journalism Review*, which covers Pacific-related media issues with special emphasis on indigenous media and media coverage of environmental issues in the region. For information on a specific island, check out Michael Ogden's Pacific Island Internet Resources.

Physical Anthropology

Annual Editions: Physical Anthropology
http://www.dushkin.com/annualeditions/0-697-37296-0.mhtml

This site offers abstracts to 44 articles reprinted in *Annual Editions*: *Physical Anthropology*. Simply reading the abstracts gives an excellent overview of the kinds of topics physical anthropologists study.

Canadian Association for Physical Anthropology Home Page
http://citd.scar.utoronto.ca/CAPA/CAPA.html

This web site is maintained by the Canadian Association for Physical Anthropology (CAPA), whose mission "is to: (1) encourage and expand the study of physical anthropology in Canada (2) promote an appreciation of physical anthropology to the public, and (3) support those who are currently engaged in the field of physical anthropology." This site provides access to current and past issues of the association's newsletter, as well as a link to the "Physical Anthropology in Canada" home page, which provides links to "educational, research, funding and employment resources related to the field." In addition, this site offers a number of useful links related to the subject of physical anthropology.

Canadian Association for Physical Anthropology-Internet Resources
http://citd.scar.utoronto.ca/CAPA/Phy_Anthro_Resources/Resourc es.html

The Canadian Association for Physical Anthropology has compiled a list of Internet links to Web sites of interest to physical anthropologists. The links are listed according to the following categories: (1) evolutionary biology (2) palaeoanthropology (3) primatology (4) growth and development (5) skeletal biology, anatomy, and forensic sciences (6) human and molecular genetics; and (7) health, diseases, and demography.

Journal of Human Evolution
http://www.hbuk.co.uk/www/ideal/journals/hu.htm

"*The Journal of Human Evolution* concentrates on publishing the highest quality papers covering all aspects of human evolution. The central focus is aimed jointly at palaeoanthropological work, covering human and primate fossils, and at comparative studies of living species, including both morphological and molecular evidence." This site offers abstracts of past and current issues via IDEAL USA.

Origins of Humankind
http://www.pro-am.com/origins/

Origins of Humankind offers a variety of resources of interest to physical anthropologists. This site includes links to chat rooms, newsgroups and message boards. The "Research Center" includes a "collection of articles and references from professors, students, and other Web sites" of interest to physical anthropologists and links to online books related to physical anthropology. "Origins of Humankind" offers an overview of four controversial theories: (1) Helpless as a Baby Theory (2) Out of Africa vs. Multiregionalism (3) Neanderthals (Our Ancestors or Not); and (4) The Independent Birth of Organisms. In addition, there is a list of links to Web sites related to the topic of human origins.

Physical Anthropology
http://www.ed.uiuc.edu/students/b-sklar/physicalsection.html

As part of a larger Web site named *Into the World of Anthropology* Bonnie Faith Sklar at the University of Illinois at Urbana-Champaign gives an overview of physical or biological anthropology.

Talk.Origins Archive
http://www.talkorigins.org

Talk.Origins Archive posts articles and essays exploring "the creationism/evolution controversy from a *mainstream* scientific perspective." The archive includes a list of frequently asked questions (and answers) about evolution in general such as, "Don't you have to be an atheist to accept evolution?" "If evolution is true, then why are there so many gaps in the fossil record?" and "Didn't Darwin renounce evolution on his death bed?" There are FAQs on the subjects of creationism, age of the earth, flood geology, catastrophism, and debates. There is also an excellent overview essay, "Introduction to Evolutionary Biology," by Chris Colby.

Primates (Nonhuman)

African Primates at Home
http://www.indiana.edu/~primate/primates.html

M.K. Holder at the University of Indiana posts photographs of the primates he studies on their home turf in East Africa.

Gorilla Home Page
http://www.cs.ukc.ac.uk/people/staff/ms3/gorillas

Mark Scahill at the University of Kent at Canterbury maintains the "Gorilla Home Page." Everything you ever wanted to know about gorillas is available at this site. Its featured contents include: "News on Mountain Gorillas," "Answers and Questions on Mountain Gorillas," "Gorilla Pictures" (offered only on Netscape), "Organizations News on Gorillas," "Gorilla Background," "Gorilla Behaviour," and "Gorilla Habitat." This site also provides links to relevant Web sites and information about the Virtual Gorilla Project being developed by researchers from the Georgia Institute of Technology and staff from Zoo Atlanta.

Primate Info Net (PIN)
http://www.primate.wisc.edu/pin/

Primate Info Net, maintained by the Wisconsin Regional Primate Research Center at the University of Wisconsin, is a Web site for those interested in the field of primatology. There is a variety of information resources available including links to general information about primates, an overview of animal welfare legislation and policies, the latest news on primates as endangered species, and "WRPRC Audiovisual Service," a collection of audio-visual records of nonhuman primates. Also of interest is "AskPrimate," an "e-mail-based international reference service for questions dealing with primates, primate organizations, or individuals in primatology."

Refugees

Refugees International
http://www.refintl.org/

Refugees International, founded in 1979, is an independent organization based in Washington, D.C. "heavily reliant on the support of committed and concerned individuals." The organization seeks to give governments and the UN early warnings about mass exoduses of refugees and to mobilize them to take action. In the last four years, Refugees International has responded to approximately thirty mass exodus crises, including calls from "Kurds stranded along the mountainous Turkish border, Burmese forced to flee to Bangladesh, war victims in Bosnia, Africans fleeing strife and famine in Liberia, Ethiopia, and Somalia, and Rwandans surging into Tanzania and Zaire." At the Web site you can access background information on

refugee crises by region of the world and the latest news and
developments related to new and ongoing refugee crises.

United Nations High Commissioner for Refugees
http://www.unhcr.ch/

This site provides "reliable and current information and analysis on all
aspects relating to refugees and displaced persons, including their
countries of origin, legal instruments, human rights, minorities,
situations of conflict, and conflict resolution."

Religion

Descriptions of 57 Religions, Faith Groups & Ethical Systems
http://web.canlink.com/ocrt/var_rel.htm

As the title suggests this Web site offers descriptions of 57 religions,
faith groups, and ethical systems. The 57 descriptions are broken down
into the following categories: 1) Long established major world religions
(e.g., Buddhism, Judaism, and Christianity) 2) Small, non-Christian
religions (e.g., Hare Krishna and Unitarian Universalism)
3) Destructive faith groups (e.g., The Family and Branch Dividians)
and 4) Other ethical groups, religions and spiritual paths. This Web site
is supported by the Ontario Consultants on Religious Tolerance whose
aims are to promote tolerance of minority religions, offer useful
information on controversial religious topics, and expose hatred and
misinformation about any religion.

Religious and Sacred Texts
http://Webpages.marshall.edu/~wiley6/rast.htmlx

The Religious and Sacred Texts Web site compiles links to various
texts and resources on the Internet to help interested parties explore the
history, thoughts, and writings of various religions from around the
world. Categories listed include Apocryphal texts, Islamic texts, Hindu
texts, the Analects of Confucius, Mormon texts, Taoist texts, World
Scripture, Bahai texts, Sikh texts, The Egyptian Book of the Dead,
Gnostic texts, Zen texts, texts by Early Christian Fathers, Zoroastrian
texts, Divrei Torah, The Urantia Book, Ethiopian Texts, and medieval
texts.

Shamanism—Frequently Asked Questions (FAQ)
http://lucy.ukc.ac.uk/cgi-bin/makehtml?Papers/shaman_FAQ

This site gives a general overview on the subject of Shamanism by answering ten frequently asked questions including "What is Shamanism?" and "What is Shamanic Ecstasy?" There is also information on "Becoming a Shaman," "The Role of Trauma in the Development of a Shaman," "The Relationship Between Shamanic Traditions and Culture," "The Role of Shamanic Ecstasy," "The Origin of the Term Shamanism," and "Roles of the Shaman."

World Scripture: A Comparative Anthology of Sacred Texts
http://www.rain.org/~origin/ws.html

The International Religious Foundation is an organization dedicated to promoting world peace through interreligious dialogue and cooperation. Select "Introduction" for more information on the purpose of the project. The foundation has posted the scriptures of several of the major world religions according to how each religion views (1) ultimate reality (2) divine law, truth, and cosmic principles (3) the purpose of human life (4) life beyond death, and (5) the human condition, as well as 16 other topics.

Scandinavia

The Society for the Advancement of Scandinavian Study
http://www.byu.edu/sasslink

"The Society for the Advancement of Scandinavian Study (SASS) is an association of scholars and others interested in the cultures of the Nordic countries" founded in 1911 with the goal of promoting Scandinavian study, research, and instruction in America, and fostering relations "between persons interested in Scandinavian studies in North America and elsewhere." Current and past issues of *Scandinavian Studies* are available to be downloaded, and the current and past issues of *SASS News & Notes* are available online. The SASS has also compiled a list of Scandinavian Resources by Country for Denmark, Faroe Islands, Finland (including Sami nation in Finland), Greenland, Iceland, Norway, and Sweden.

Sections/Interest Groups

Sections/Interest Groups
http://www.ameranthassn.org/sctigs.htm

Links to the 30 plus sections/interest groups within the American
Anthropological Association are listed. The following is a listing of the
subsections/associations and their URL endings, which may be directly
accessed at: **http://www.ameranthassn.org/**

American Ethnological Society	**aes.htm**
Anthropology and Environment Section	**ae.htm**
Archaeology Division	**ad.htm**
Association for Africanist Anthropology	**afaa.htm**
Association of Black Anthropologists	**aba.htm**
Association for Feminist Anthropology	**afa.htm**
Association of Latina and Latino Anthropologists	**alla.htm**
Association for Political and Legal Anthropology	**apla.htm**
Association of Senior Anthropologists	**asa.htm**
Biological Anthropology Section	**bas.htm**
Central States Anthropological Society	**csas.htm**
Council on Anthropology and Education	**cae.htm**
Council for General Anthropology	**cga.htm**
Council for Museum Anthropology	**cma.htm**
Council on Nutritional Anthropology	**can.htm**
Culture and Agriculture	**cag.htm**
Middle East Section	**mes.htm**
National Association for the Practice of Anthropology	**napa.htm**
National Association of Student Anthropologists	**nasa.htm**
Society for Anthropology in Community Colleges	**sacc.htm**
Society for the Anthropology of Consciousness	**sac.htm**
Society for the Anthropology of Europe	**sae.htm**
Society for the Anthropology of North America	**sana.htm**
Society for the Anthropology of Work	**saw.htm**
Society for Cultural Anthropology	**sca.htm**
Society for Humanistic Anthropology	**sha.htm**
Society for Latin American Anthropology	**slaa.htm**
Society for Linguistic Anthropology	**sla.htm**

Society for Medical Anthropology	**sma.htm**
Society for Psychological Anthropology	**spa.htm**
Society for Urban Anthropology	**sua.htm**
Society for Visual Anthropology	**sva.htm**

Each site gives information such as the bylaws, officers and publications for each section/interest group listed.

Socio-Cultural Research Methods

The Anthropologist in the Field
http://www.truman.edu/academics/ss/faculty/tamakoshil/field.html

Laura Tamakoshi and Brian Cross at Truman State University prepared this guide to fieldwork research. It has 4 major sections: (1) planning, (2) method, (3) writing, and (4) reference. Each of these four sections has several subsections. For example the planning section includes information regarding proposals, preparation, choosing a field site, and travel arrangements.

The Center for Anthropology and Science Communications
http://chimera.acs.ttu.edu/~wurlr/anthro.html

The Center for Anthropology and Science Communications is a media resource for finding anthropologists and for communicating anthropology "through the media, the Internet, news and information services." Of particular interest is the section on "media anthropology," which gives a short history of the term, the "AAA Checklist for Easy and Effective Press," suggestions for "The Effective Press Release" and for handling television interviews.

Center for Social Anthropology and Computing (CSAC)
http://lucy.ukc.ac.uk

The University of Kent at Canterbury sponsors the CSAS Web site. CSAS aims to serve the worldwide anthropology community and to advance anthropology by offering information resources, developing new methods for researching anthropological problems, and promoting the use of computer technology in anthropological research. Of particular interest on this Web site is the CSAC Studies in Anthropology Vol. 11, which offers full online text of various anthropological papers which include such topics as "Indigenous Knowledge of the Rainforest" and "City Dweller Perceptions of

African Forests." These papers can be accessed directly at **http://lucy.ukc.ac.uk/CSACSIA/Research.html**. Also included in this document is online text of papers sponsored by the CSAC. Manuscripts include "Kinship, Marriage and Residence—A Database Approach" which describes how computers have assisted anthropologists studying complex subjects such as kinship. This paper may be accessed directly at **http://lucy.ukc.ac.uk:80/CSACSIA/Vol11/Papers/index.html**.

Cultural Anthropology Methods (CAM)
http://www.lawrence.edu/~bradleyc/cam.html

The journal *Cultural Anthropology Methods* publishes articles related to qualitative and quantitative methods in anthropology. The table of contents for all issues of CAM published since 1989 are online. The texts of three articles are online. One is on ethnographic sampling, a second is about cross-cultural research, and a third is a Guttman scale analysis of Matsigenka Men's Manufacturing Skills.

Culture of the Net (Research on)
http://www.vianet.net.au/~timn/thesis/index.html

This anthropology masters thesis by Tim North is an excellent example of ethnographic research. North argues that a new culture has emerged from the ever-growing population of Internet users and that the Internet has become a society with its own distinct culture. He describes that culture, emphasizing its impact on newcomers and the process by which they become enculturated. North presents more than the end product of his ethnographic research. He describes each step of the research process, explaining how he did his research. This is helpful for those doing their first research proposal or literature review, or who need advice about how to gain entree, take notes, or write up research results.

Folklife and Fieldwork (Guide)
http://lcweb.loc.gov/folklife/fieldwk.html

The American Folklife Center gives online access to a folklife fieldwork guide, *A Layman's Introduction to Field Techniques*, by Peer Bartes. There is a brief introduction to folklife followed by a review of a fieldwork project in three parts: 1) preparation 2) fieldwork itself, and 3) processing the material collected.

Getting Started in Oral Tradition Research—A Manual
http://tailpipe.learnnet.nt.ca/pwnhc/

The Prince of Wales Northern Heritage Centre supports the Gwich'in Social and Cultural Institute (GSC). The Institute documents Gwich'in oral history and traditional knowledge. A manual outlining the basic principles of oral tradition research has been posted. The manual defines oral tradition, written tradition, and traditional knowledge. It also gives advice on preparing for interviews, interviewing, processing information, and reporting results.

Problems with Anthropologists' Use of Libraries
ftp://vela.acs.oakland.edu/pub/anthap/Problems_with_anthropologists_use_of_libraries

Andrew Brenan, III, College of Library and Information Sciences (Drexel University) prepared "The Problems with Anthropologists' Use of Libraries." Brenen maintains that the scope and breadth of anthropology, in combination with library classification systems present special problems to anthropologists seeking to locate and retrieve relevant information.

Qualitative Research in Information Systems
http://www.aukland.ac.nz/msis/isworld

This site provides an excellent overview of qualitative research for those students interested in learning about its methods and applications. It begins with a comparison between qualitative and quantitative research methods and offers a basic definition of triangulation (an approach to social research that combines quantitative and qualitative research). The emphasis is on the methods of qualitative research: case study research, critical social theory, ethnographic research, grounded theory and interpretive research, narrative and metaphor, and actions research. For each method, you will find a brief definition and a list of selected references for further reading.

Review and Evaluation of Networked Sources
http://www.artsci.wustl.edu/~anthro/ca/papers/schwimmer/intro.html

This review and evaluation, originally published in *Current Anthropology*, was written by Brian Schwimmer of the Anthropology Department at the University of Manitoba with the goal of bringing the Internet "to the attention of the wider community, to assess the current scope of networked resources for anthropology, and to discuss opportunities and challenges for future development." The author gives a history of the Internet, including an overview of the ways the Internet is being used and the numerous anthropological resources on the Internet such as discussion groups, research collections, scholarly journals and anthropology departments. The author explains the potential benefits of the Internet to anthropology and urges more anthropologists to make use of this resource.

South America

Archaeology Research in Peru
http://members.aol.com/OwenBruce/index.htm

Dr. Bruce Owen maintains this site, which provides "full browseable text, abstracts, references, and selected graphics from archaeological research papers presented by Bruce Owen at academic conferences, plus a picture gallery of archaeological ceramics and other information."

Study Abroad

Archaeological Fieldwork Opportunities
http://durendal.cit.cornell.edu/TestPit.html

This site is maintained by the Archaeological Institute of America at Cornell University. It provides a frequently updated list of opportunities for "hands on" experience in the field of archaeology. Choose a region of the world where you would like to do fieldwork: North America, Mexico, Central America, the Caribbean, the Middle East, Africa, Europe, Asia, Australia, New Zealand and the Pacific, or South America. Within each region are specific locations where fieldwork is being done. The site also gives pertinent information regarding food and lodging, skills required to participate in fieldwork projects, expenses, and the names of people to contact.

Cultural Immersion
http://www.nrcsa.com/

The National Registration Center for Study Abroad gives information about immersion classes in 30 different countries. The online information covers program descriptions, dates, and fees.

Semester at Sea's Home Page on CampusNET
http://campus.net/educat/semester/

"The Semester at Sea is a floating university allowing students to experience diverse cultures while getting credit from the University of Pittsburgh." This page provides access to a general overview of the program, the mission statement, campus information, and information on the student body, enrollment, the academic program, the faculty, courses, and so on.

Study Abroad and Summer Study
http://www.uky.edu/ArtsSciences/Classics/summer.html

For students interested in studying, traveling, or working abroad, this University of Kentucky (U.K.) Web site offers information about study abroad programs. Programs are set up for a summer, a semester, or an entire year, and correspondence courses are also offered. In addition to information about its own study-abroad opportunities, there are links to Web sites offering other kinds of useful information for the student traveler. Of particular interest to students interested in archaeology are links to Web sites related to excavation projects. Examples include excavations in Eleusis, Sepphoris, Israel, and Roman Carthage.

Study Abroad Home Page
http://www.studyabroad.com/

This site is a resource for students to learn about study-abroad programs in 65 countries. Read the document "Consumer Information" before making any decisions about a program.

Study/Work Abroad

The Bureau of Applied Research in Anthropology
http://wacky.ccit.arizona.edu/~bara/new0001.html

Are you looking for valuable internship opportunities? If you are in the advanced stages of your undergraduate education you many want to consider internship opportunities available through the Bureau of Applied Research in Anthropology (BARA). BARA's internships contribute "to the betterment of human populations, communities, and individuals through scholarship, advocacy and practice." Organizations that support BARA internships include the World Bank, the United States Department of Energy, the National Park Service, the Bureau of Reclamation, and U.S. AID—Women in Development Office. Internships are available summer, fall, and winter.

Earthwatch
http://gaia.earthwatch.org/

In the past 20 years, Earthwatch, a non-profit organization, has mobilized 1,845 projects in 109 countries. They expect 600 teachers and students to go on field expeditions in 1997. At this site, read about the new 1997 expeditions such as House of the Badlands, an archaeological exploration, and Mexican Art of Building, an artistic and architectural study of cultural and historic areas of Mexico. If this interests you, check out the expeditions catalogue for information on participation and membership (expedition costs range from $600 to $2,200, excluding airfare). Other exciting Earthwatch features include the college credit program, events calendar, employment opportunities, project results, and virtual field trips.

Peace Corps
http://www.peacecorps.gov/

Peace Corps volunteers work in Africa, Asia-Pacific, Inter-America and the Caribbean, Eastern Europe, and the Mediterranean in the areas of agriculture, education, forestry, health, engineering, skilled trades, business, the environment, urban planning, youth development, and the teaching of English for use in commerce and technology. This site gives information about the Peace Corps, becoming a Peace Corps volunteer, the places where Peace Corps volunteers work, and the Peace Corps global education program (which contains letters and interviews with Peace Corps volunteers).

Voluntary Service Overseas
http://www.oneworld.org/vso/

The Voluntary Service Overseas is an organization that recruits people between the ages of 20 and 70 to work in developing countries. This page answers questions about the program's goals, discusses volunteering, describes job openings, and gives general information about the program.

Style Guides

American Anthropological Association Style Guide
http://www.ameranthassn.org/aaastyle.htm

Society for American Archaeology Style Guide
http://www.saa.org/Publications/StyleGuide/styframe.html

Of particular interest to student researchers are the links "Editor's and Author's Responsibilities" and "Textual Elements." "Textual Elements" offers rules for consistently handling a variety of writing decisions specific to archaeology.

Urbanization

World Urbanization Prospects
gopher://gopher.undp.org/00/ungophers/popin/wdtrends/urban

The United Nations report *World Urbanization Projects, the 1994 Revision* gives estimates and projections of urban, rural, and city populations. For each country and major geographical region the UN lists the number of people living in areas defined as urban and rural and projects those numbers to the year 2025. It also lists the percentages of the population living in urban areas in 1994 and projected to 2025.

White House Press Releases

Today's Press Releases from the White House
http://library.whitehouse.gov/PressReleases-plain.cgi

This site contains all of the press releases coming directly from the White House for the current day. The press releases typically are related to speeches made by the president, first lady, and members of the White House staff. The site also provides access to yesterday's press releases. In addition to White House press releases, there are daily press briefings from the White House press secretary. They can be found at **http://library.whitehouse.gov/Briefings-plain.cgi**.

World as a Unit

World Factbook
http://www.odci.gov/cia/publications/nsolo/factbook/w.htm

This 1996 CIA World Factbook includes a section that considers the world as a unit. For example, it gives the unemployment rate, population, and total fertility for the world.

Part II

General Reference

Abbreviations

Abbreviations for International Organizations and Groups
http://www.ic.gov/cia/publications/nsolo/wfb-appa.htm

Do you need to know what a particular abbreviation stands for? Or would you like to know the abbreviation of an organization for a project or paper? This site lists accepted abbreviations for international organizations and groups starting with the Arab Bank for Economic Development in Africa (ABEDA) and ending with the Zangger Committee.

Books

Amazon.com Books! Earth's Biggest Bookstore
http://www.amazon.com/

If you are a book lover, this site is a must-see. Amazon.com is an online book order "catalogue" that lists more than 2.5 million titles from the "hard-to-find" to the "easy-to-find" at discount prices (40% off bestsellers, 10% off hardcovers, 10% off paperbacks, and special deals in certain genres such as science fiction and mystery). Search for books by author, title, or subject or browse the shelves under categories such as bestsellers, award winners, and editors' favorites.

Main Online Books Page
http://www.cs.cmu.edu/Web/books.html

This site is an index of over 1,800 online books that you can browse by author or title. Some foreign language materials are available, and some books of particular interest to anthropologists are also listed. Keep in mind that books can be listed only if someone has taken the time to put them online.

Calculators

Calculators Online
http://www-sci.lib.uci.edu/HSG/RefCalculators.html

This site is a list of calculators for almost everything you can imagine. You can figure out the maximum hull speed on your sailboat, determine your financial net worth, calculate your body mass, do simple and complex math, and much more.

Calendars

Calendar Generator
http://www.stud.unit.no/USERBIN/steffent/kalender.pl?+1996

Are you interested in knowing what day your birthday will be on in the year 2005? Or do you need to know what day of the week it was when Abraham Lincoln was born on February 12, 1809? You can submit a year between 1754 and 3000 to generate a 12-month calendar for that year.

Census Bureau

Census Bureau Press Releases
http://www.census.gov/Press-Release/www

The press releases at this site can be searched by subject or by date. Many of the press releases announce new statistics related to a wide range of subjects, from aging to national population estimates.

Census 2000 Press Releases
http://www.census.gov/Press-Release/www/2000.html

This Web site contains Census Bureau press releases relating to Census 2000. Press releases announce plans for making the census simpler, less expensive, and more accurate and summarize recommendations made by various advisory committees. Most of the press releases relate to the issue of racial and ethnic classification and to plans to reach populations that have traditionally been undercounted.

Demographic and Population Contacts at the Census Bureau
http://www.census.gov/contacts/www/c-demopop.html

Do you need information from the Census Bureau but are unsure of where to look for it? This site lists the names and phone numbers of people by department at the Census Bureau who can help you find information on topics ranging from age structures to voter characteristics.

United States Bureau of the Census
http://www.census.gov/

The Bureau of the Census is a general-purpose federal agency that collects, tabulates, and publishes a wide variety of statistical data about the people and economy of the United States. The statistical results of the censuses, surveys, and other Census Bureau programs are available to the public.

City-Level Information (U.S. and World Cities)

CityNet
http://www.city.net/

This page is aimed at the traveler and offers information on 2,333 U.S. and international cities. It lists links to the most popular U.S. and international cities.

County and City Data Books
http://www.lib.virginia.edu/socsci/ccdb/city94.html

The University of Virginia Social Sciences Data Center provides access to the 1994 *County and City Data Book*. At this URL city-level information is available on the foreign-born population, family and nonfamily households, number of vehicles per household, and so on. There are approximately 240 data tables from which to select.

Top City Rankings
http://www.census.gov/stat_abstract/ccdb.html

This Census Bureau site contains tables in which U.S. cities are ranked according to factors such as percentage of foreign born residents, population size, percentage of workers using public transportation, and so on.

USA CityLink
http://banzai.neosoft.com/citylink/

The USA CityLink is a collaborative project that claims to offer the most comprehensive list of links to city and state Web sites. Many U.S. cities participate in this project. CityLink requires that 90 percent of the information each city and state links to the site must be about the state or city, and it must be useful to someone planning to travel to or visit the area. Examples of useful information include school system profiles, historical overviews, and descriptions of interesting tourist attractions and cultural events.

Congress

Almanac of American Politics
http://politicsusa.com/PoliticsUSA/resources/almanac/

The *National Journal* maintains this site, which lists U.S. representatives and senators for each state along with some background information on each person. It also gives information on the senators and representatives who rank highest in fund-raising and spending, who receive the most PAC and individual contributions, and who have the most cash on hand.

Connecting with People Via the Internet

College E-mail Addresses
http://www.qucis.queensu.ca/FAQs/email/college.html

Looking for an old roommate? This site gives you information about how to search colleges from around the country for student and faculty e-mail addresses. In order to search for an e-mail address you must: (1) choose a specific college name from which to search (2) select the database that includes that college's name (the colleges are listed alphabetically), and (3) page down until you find the name of the college you are looking for (remember, not all colleges are listed.) When you find the college you are interested in, read the information below the name, this will tell you how the e-mail addresses at that school are configured. (First time users should visit the General Information section on the home page to get an idea of how the explanations are written.) For example, if I were looking for Mary K. Smith at SUNY Oswego, I would select database part 6, page down to SUNY Oswego, and by following their format, e-mail to Msmith@Oswego.edu. In addition, some colleges allow you to search their database directly for an e-mail or home address.

CyberFriends
http://cyberfriends.com

The purpose of CyberFriends is to provide an easy way for people sharing similar interests and professions to meet on the Internet. You simply fill out an application, which asks approximately 20 optional and required questions (age, sex, nationality, hobbies, personal philosophy, and so on). In two or three weeks your application will be posted free of charge. In the meantime you can search CyberFriends listings for profiles and e-mail addresses for the names of people with whom you might like to correspond.

Find a Person/A Business/A Group
http://www.switchboard.com/bin/cgiqa.dll?MEM=1

Switchboard Opportunities sponsors this searchable index for locating businesses, groups, organizations, and individuals listed in United States telephone directories. Simply plug in the information you do know about someone, i.e., last name, first name, city, and/or state. If you know only the last name, this Web site will give you name, address, and telephone number of everyone in the U.S. with that last name.

Country Information (General)

Background Notes on the Countries of the World
http://www.state.gov/www/background_notes/index.html

This site contains statistical and general information on most of the countries of the world (but not the United States) and covers geography, people, education, economics, and membership in international organizations.

Country Studies
http://lcweb2.loc.gov/frd/cs/country.html

This site gives access to book-length information on Ethiopia, China, Egypt, Indonesia, Israel, Japan, Philippines, Singapore, Somalia, South Korea, and Yugoslavia. It is a comprehensive source of information about all areas of life including politics, economics, religion, population, history, and culture.

Country Studies/Area Handbook Program
http://lcweb2.loc.gov/frd/cs/cshome.html

The Country Studies/Area Handbook Program is an ongoing and continuously updated series of books prepared by the Federal Research Division of the Library of Congress. There are 71 country studies online. Each country study gives a comprehensive overview of the society, geography, economy, politics, history, people, and major institutions (religion, education, health).

International Demographic Data
http://www.census.gov/ftp/pub/ipc/www/idbsum.html

This Census Bureau site includes data on the population of every country and territory in the world for 1950, 1960, 1970, 1980, 1990, and 1991-1995. Population is also projected to the year 2000, as is age-specific population size.

The World Factbook 1996
http://www.odci.gov/cia/publications/nsolo/factbook/global.htm#W

This 1996 CIA World Factbook includes a section that considers the world as a unit. For example, it gives the unemployment rate, population, and total fertility for the world.

U.S. Department of State Home Page
http://www.state.gov/

This site is an official U.S. government source. The U.S. Department of State is the main U.S. foreign affairs agency and is responsible for implementing the President's foreign policies. The Hot Spot link updates you on most recent spotlighted information concerning foreign policies, such as "Patterns of Global Terrorism" and "Earth Day." The travel link gives you information on every area in the world and the traveling requirements to get there. This site also gives useful telephone numbers and a 1996 Department Telephone Directory.

Currency Converter

Currency Converter
http://www.tcn.net/~datatel/currency.html

This Web site is a service of Switzerland-based Olsen & Associates, Ltd. Find an exchange rate on any day from 1990 to the present year. Simply type in the number of U.S. dollars you wish to exchange. Specify the currency of exchange and the date for which you what to know the exchange rate. Select "See the exchange rate."

Encyclopedias Online

Encyclopedia Smithsonian
http://www.si.edu/resource/faq/start.htm

Topics included in this encyclopedia are determined by public demand for information on a topic. As of June 1996, there were nine general topics: armed forces history, anthropology, mineral sciences, musical history, physical sciences, services, conservation of textiles, transportation history, and vertebrate zoology.

Free Internet Encyclopedia
http://clever.net/cam/encyclopedia.html

Creators of this site suggest that a more accurate name than "Free Internet Encyclopedia" is "Free Internet Encyclopedia Index" because this is an encyclopedia of information on the Internet. This encyclopedia has two divisions: Macroreference (large general topics such as Africa, court, and so on) and Microreference (short bits of information on specific topics such as asthma, Jane Austen, and so on).

Etiquette on the Net

Emoticons and Abbreviations
http://pw2.netcom.com/~jampie96/emoticons.html

Internet Terms
http://134.84.217.16/icec/training/terms.html

Netiquette
http://www.albion.com/TOC0963702513

Experts, Authorities, and Spokespersons

Yearbook of Experts, Authorities, and Spokespersons
http://www.yearbook.com/

The Broadcast Interview Source posts this Web site, which offers the addresses of experts, authorities, and spokespersons for various organizations. Search by topic or keyword. For example, the word "refugees" produced six sources of possible information, each of which included an address, a profile, and a home page as applicable.

Federal Courts

Understanding the Federal Courts
http://www.uscourts.gov/understanding_courts/899_toc.htm

Do you have questions about how the federal court system works? This site provides answers to your questions with a glossary of terms; an overview of the organization, operation, and administration of the court system; a list of the location and number of judges who sit on each court; and charts showing the structure of the federal court system and the path a case takes as it works its way through this system.

General Reference

Finding Data on the Internet: Links to Potential Story Data
http://nilesonline.com/data/

This site is maintained by journalist Robert Niles with the intention of making it easy for other journalists to find statistics and data on the Internet. The following topics are covered: basic reference data, agriculture, aviation, banks and businesses, crime, economy and population, education, energy, finding people, health, immigration, law, military, non-profits, politics, and weather. For each of these topics links to facts and information are provided. This site also provides links to the *World Fact Book*, the Library of Congress, and other sources.

Librarians' Index to the Internet
http://sunsite.berkeley.edu/InternetIndex/

The Librarians' Index to the Internet is "a searchable, annotated, subject directory of more than 2,500 Internet resources chosen for their usefulness to the public library user's information needs." The subjects indexed range from "Arts" to "Women."

Reference Center of the Internet Public Library
http://ipl.sils.umich.edu/ref/RR/

This site provides links to Internet resources on the following subjects: general reference, arts and humanities, business and economics, computers and the Internet, education, entertainment and leisure, health and medical sciences, law, government and political science, science and technology, and social sciences.

Scholarly Societies Project
http://www.lib.uwaterloo.ca/society/subjects_soc.html

The University of Waterloo Electronic Library has compiled a list of subject categories and corresponding scholarly societies with Web pages. These scholarly societies include subjects ranging from agriculture and food to women's issues. Choose the category "dance" and find at least 10 scholarly societies ranging from American Society of Aesthetics to Texas Association of Health, P.E., Recreation and Dance.

World Lecture Hall
http://www.utexas.edu/world/lecture

"The World Lecture Hall (WLH) contains links to pages created by faculty worldwide who are using the Web to deliver class materials. For example, you will find course syllabi, assignments, lecture notes, exams, class calendars, multimedia, textbooks, etc." This site contains information about online courses in disciplines ranging from Accounting to Zoology.

Historical Documents

Cultural Maps of U.S. History
http://xroads.virginia.edu/~MAP/map_hp.html

"Cultural Maps is dedicated to the graphical presentation of non-graphical information..." This site offers an "American Historical Atlas," that includes U.S. Territorial Maps from 1775 to 1920. Also included is a "Historical Geography" section that posts the paper *"Exploring the West from Monticello: A Perspective in Maps from Columbus to Lewis and Clark* from The University of Virginia's Alderman Library." In addition, Cultural Maps has compiled a list of online map collections related to U.S. history. This site is best viewed using Netscape.

Historical Letters, Documents, Essays, and Speeches
http://history.cc.ukans.edu/carrie/docs/docs_us.html

The University of Kansas has posted an extensive list of historical documents beginning with Christopher Columbus's 1494 letter to the queen and king of Spain and ending with the 1993 Freedom of Information Act.

Historical Newspapers
http://lcweb.loc.gov/global/ncp/extnewsp.html#hist

This private collection of historical newspapers focuses on the early American experience, including the Colonial period, the Revolution, and the presidencies of Washington and Jefferson.

Historical Photographs
http://www.cmp.ucr.edu/exhibitions/netex_history_intro.html

The University of California at Riverside/California Museum of Photography, "devoted to photography as both art and social document, is one of the most significant photographic museums in the United States." This site offers numerous historical photographs, including "Ellis Island," "Russia Before the Revolution" and "Trains."

National Archives and Records Administration
http://www.nara.gov/nara/whatsnew.html

The National Archives and Records Administration is an independent federal agency that maintains famous historical documents and enables people to view these documents. This site provides links to new NARA exhibitions and the *Federal Register*.

Search the White House Virtual Library
http://www.whitehouse.gov/WH/html/library-plain.html

This site allows users to search the White House databases for White House documents, radio addresses of the president, executive orders, and White House photographs. It is also possible to browse some historical national documents.

U.S. Historical Documents
gopher://wiretap.spies.com/11/Gov/US-History

This site contains the text of a number of important documents beginning with the Declaration of Arms in 1775 and ending with the U.S. State Department's release of the text of the agreements reached at the 1944 Yalta Conference attended by Roosevelt, Churchill, and Stalin (see "World War II Documents").

Libraries

Library of Congress Home Page
http://lcweb.loc.gov/

This is a source for links to publications, foreign and U.S. newspapers, the government, Congress, copyright laws and procedures, events and exhibits, and special collections.

State Library and Web Listings
http://www.state.wi.us/0/agencies/dpi/www/statelib.html

The Wisconsin Department of Public Instruction posts this list of hypertext links to state libraries. Some of the libraries give only basic information such as their hours and phone numbers, access to library catalogs and resources, as well as convention and visitor's bureau information, state job bulletins, and legal information.

Maps

Cultural Maps of U.S. History
http://xroads.virginia.edu/~MAP/map_hp.html

"Cultural Maps is dedicated to the graphical presentation of non-graphical information…" This site offers an "American Historical Atlas," that includes U.S. Territorial Maps from 1775 to 1920. Also included is a "Historical Geography" section that posts the paper *"Exploring the West from Monticello: A Perspective in Maps from Columbus to Lewis and Clark* from the University of Virginia's Alderman Library." In addition, Cultural Maps has compiled a list of online map collections related to U.S. history. This site is best viewed using Netscape.

MapQuest! Interactive Atlas
http://www.mapquest.com

Mapquest posts the Interactive Atlas, an online service that allows users access to county-level and city-level maps from over six continents. This atlas allows you to enter a street address along with its city, state, and zip code and to access a map of that address and surrounding streets and landmarks. A one-time, free registration is required, which allows you to save and store maps for later use.

Maps in the News
http://www-map.lib.umn.edu/news.html

The John R. Borchert Library of the University of Minnesota posts this site, which provides links to maps of regions that are in the news because of conflict or disaster. The number and quality of maps available varies by region.

Perry-Castaneda Library
**http://www.lib.utexas.edu/Libs/PCL/Map_collection/Map_collectio
n.html**

The Perry-Castañeda Library Map Collection, sponsored by the University of Texas at Austin, "holds more than 230,000 maps covering every area of the world." This site offers electronic maps of various regions of the world, ranging from Africa to Texas; electronic maps of the world; and historical maps. This site must be viewed using Netscape.

Media Contacts

Media List
http://link.tsl.state.tx.us/.dir/ready.dir/.files/medialist

This site provides a list of e-mail addresses for newspapers, magazines, TV stations, and other media outlets that accept electronic submissions. This is a convenient method for writing letters or contacting media services with comments or for subscription information. Foreign news services are represented here as well.

Welcome to DIGEX
http://www.digex.net/

This National Press Club Web site offers a directory of news sources, including links to various agencies, magazines, and schools. It is designed for reporters and editors who need to find background information quickly for a story and the names of key contacts. The resources are grouped into subjects that begin with "Abortion and Reproductive Rights" and end with "Workplace Trends and Issues."

Media-Watch Resources

Media Watchdog
http://theory.lcs.mit.edu/~mernst/media

This site compiles online media-watch resources, including organizations, articles, censorship material, and other resources. The "Top Censored Stories" section is a good source of information on issues such as child labor, nuclear weapons, and the Internet.

Movies

The Internet Movie Database Tour
http://us.imdb.com/tour.html

This Web site defies brief description. We suggest that you take the Internet Movie Database Tour, which will give you a feel for the wide rage of information housed at this site. There are more than a million entries covering 300,000 people, from actors/actresses to sound recording directors. There are plot summaries, FAQs, well-known quotations, trivia, and much more.

Music

HitsWorld
http://www.hitsworld.com/

Hitsworld is a Web site that devotes coverage to top 5 and top 100 music charts. The site includes album reviews (and invites interested parties to submit reviews), Internet top 30 lists, and international charts.

News

CReAte Your Own Newspaper (CRAYON)
http://crayon.net/

CRAYON is a service maintained by Pressence Incorporated for managing news. After completing a free registration, users select the news sources from which they want to draw information. News sources are available at the international (such as *This Week in Germany*), national (such as *USA Today*), and local (such as *The Detroit News*) levels. Users may select information to be taken from specific sections, such as Sports or Weather, of the papers they choose.

Users assign a name and motto to their paper and are given a URL address where they can read their paper daily. A graphical browser is required to access this site.

Documents in the News
http://www.lib.umich.edu/libhome/Documents.center/docnews.html

This frequently updated site contains government documents relating to current news events. The University of Michigan Documents Center reports on government actions that make the news and on official government responses to domestic and international events such as the Montana Freemen standoff and the bombing of the U.S. military compound in Saudi Arabia. Documents in the news are also available for 1995.

Ecola's Newsstand
http://www.ecola.com/news/

Ecola's Newsstand provides links to 1,811 (and counting) English-language newspapers, magazines, and computer-related publications from around the world.

Foreign Service Journal
http://www.afsa.org/fsj/index.html

The *Foreign Service Journal*, a monthly magazine of the American Foreign Service Association, is aimed at active and retired foreign service employees and at those interested in international diplomacy and U.S. foreign policy. Foreign affairs professionals, Foreign Service officers, and diplomatic correspondents write the articles for the journals. Some examples of titles of featured articles include "Has the U.S. Abandoned Its 'Best Friend' in Africa During 8-Year Civil War?" "Expanding U.S. Influence: After the Fall of USSR, America Moves Quickly to Establish Posts," and "Eulogy for a Consulate: Tiny U.S. Post Shuts Down in Bilbao After Two Centuries of American Presence." Past and present issues are available for online viewing.

Hot News/Hot Research
http://www.poynter.org/hr/hr_intro.htm

Do you find that some news stories are hard to understand because you lack background information? The Poynter Institute for Media Studies, a non-profit journalism school in St. Petersburg, Florida, has created a Web site to help you understand the context behind the headline news. It offers links to Internet sites that will broaden your knowledge on a topic. For example, suppose you wanted to go beyond the headlines for more information on the 1996 bomb explosion at the U.S. Air Force base in Saudi Arabia. The Poynter Institute presents links that will take you to (1) President Clinton's remarks (2) the U.S. Air Force Web site (3) press releases from the Defense Department (4) a map of Saudi Arabia (5) the 1995 World Factbook for background material on Saudi Arabia, and (6) the Saudi Arabia embassy.

Library of Congress Foreign Newspapers
http://lcweb.loc.gov/global/ncp/oltitles.html#fornx

On this site the newspapers are listed alphabetically. Papers range in title form *The Age* (Melbourne, Australia) to *Weekly Mail and Guardian* (Johannesburg, South Africa). Other countries with newspapers represented include Canada, Ecuador, India, Italy, Mexico, Nepal, Russia, and Sweden. Some of the newspapers are in English.

Los Angeles Times
http://www.latimes.com/

Network News

The following sites provide links to television networks. Daily programming as well as news highlights can be found at these sites.

ABC
http://www.abc.com/

CBS
http://www.cbs.com/

CNN Interactive
http://www.cnn.com/

NBC
http://www.nbc.com/

New York Times
http://www.nytimes.com/

In order to read *The New York Times* online, you must register the first time you visit the site. At the moment it is free.

News from Reuters Online
http://www.yahoo.com/headlines/

Newspaper Listing—Worldwide
http://www.dds.nl/~kidon/papers.html

This site provides links to long list of foreign newspapers. Most of the newspapers are in their respective languages, but some are in English.

Public Broadcasting Service
http://www.pbs.org

This is the home page of the Public Broadcasting Service. This is an amazing resource for in-depth coverage of headline news and social and cultural issues in general. The quality of the material on this site defies simple summary. Start with the "Online Newshour" and browse its "past programs" and "essays and dialogues." Plug in keywords of interest to anthropologists such as specific country names, culture, archaeology, Native Americans, language, etc.

State News
http://www.usatoday.com/news/states/ns1.htm

USA Today presents a significant news event for each of the 50 states.

This Week's Magazine
http://pathfinder.com/@@At7@ngYAxeegunTi/time/magazine/domestic/toc/latest.html

Time Daily
http://www.pathfinder.com/@@TLDE1QYAxeeEZGze/time/daily

Today in History
http://www.historychannel.com/today/

USA Today
http://www.usatoday.com/

Washington Post
http://www.washingtonpost.com/

Publications Online

Academic Press Journal Sites
http://www.apnet.com/www/journal/

Academic Press has compiled a list of its academic journals with Web sites on the Internet. The list is presented alphabetically and according to subject.

Monster Magazine List
http://www.enews.com/monster

This is an extensive list of online magazines. If you know the title of the magazine you are looking for, use the search option. If you do not know the title, select "All Titles." If you need to know the names of magazines that cover a general topic, browse the subject headings. Not all of the magazines represented on this site are free, and some require that you subscribe in order to read them.

New Jour
http://gort.ucsd.edu/newjour/

This site lists new journals and newsletters that have become available on the Internet in the past six months.

Register of Leading Social Sciences Electronic Journals
http://www.clas.ufl.edu/users/gthursby/socsci/ejournal.htm

This site compiles the leading online journals of value to researchers in the social sciences and humanities. Select the link "Alphabetical List of the Topics" and 19 screens of topics appear for you to choose from. Examples of topics are transportation, religion, and AIDS.

Scholarly Journals Distributed Via the Web
http://info.lib.uh.edu/wj/webjour.html

University of Houston Libraries provide links to Web-based English-language scholarly journals that require no user registration fees.

Study Skills

ERIC Digests
http://www.ed.gov/databases/ERIC.Digests/

ERIC is a clearinghouse for educational material. The following are selected ERIC publications related to study skills, and the college experience. Use the numbers to the left of the titles listed below followed by .html to complete the URL address above (e.g. http://www.ed.gov/databases/ERIC_Digests/**ed325659.html**).

Study Skills
250694 Qualities of Effective Writing Programs
250696 Vocabulary
291205 Critical Presentation Skills—Research to Practice
296347 Audience Awareness: When and How Does It Develop?
300805 Note-Taking: What Do We Know About the Benefits?
301143 Learning Styles
302558 Improving Your Test-Taking Skills
318039 How to "Read" Television: Teaching Students to View TV Critically
327216 Information Skills for an Information Society: A Review
326304 How Can We Teach Critical Thinking?
372756 Information Literacy in an Information Society
385613 Making the A: How to Study for Tests in College
284510 Self-Study in Higher Education: The Path to Excellence
266339 Selecting a College: A Checklist Approach
284514 Student Stress: Effects and Solutions
284526 Reducing Stress Among Students
286938 Alternatives to Standardized Tests
351079 First-Generation College Students

Style Guides

A Guide for Writing Research Papers Based on Modern Language Association Documentation
http://155.43.225.30/mla.htm

This guide covers the various stages of the research process with advice on how to gather material, keep track of sources, take notes, document and cite references, and so on. There is also an informative article on plagiarism and examples of how to cite print and electronic references.

Bibliographic Formats for Citing Electronic Information
http://www.uvm.edu/~crane/estyles/

Do you have questions about how to cite information from the World Wide Web? This site covers the MLA and APA citation formats for electronic information. It presents clear examples for almost any type of electronic resources. APA stands for American Psychological Association and MLA stands for Modern Language Association, and both formats are commonly used across many academic disciplines.

Elements of Style
http://www.columbia.edu/acis/bartleby/strunk/

This is a guide to the proper use of the English language, with special focus on commonly misused words and expressions. It focuses on the rules of usage and writing principles most commonly violated.

Grammar Handbook
http://www.english.uiuc.edu/cws/wworkshop/writer.html

Written by students at the University of Illinois, this handbook covers the parts of speech, phrases, clauses, sentences and sentence elements, and common usage problems. The section on common usage problems (when to use a colon versus a semicolon, where in a sentence to place modifiers) is especially useful for fine-tuning writing assignments.

Online Resources for Writers
http://www.ume.maine.edu/%7Ewcenter/resource.html

This site gives links to a wide range of writing resources on the Internet including grammar, familiar quotations, dictionaries, thesauri, foreign-language dictionaries, citation guides, English as a second language, composition and rhetoric, and much more.

Purdue Online Writing Laboratory
http://owl.english.purdue.edu

The Purdue Online Writing Laboratory is a must for anyone writing a research paper. It takes you through the steps of writing a paper, from developing an outline to using statistics effectively. Paraphrasing, grammar, and citation formats are also covered at this site. There is even an exercise in which you can practice the fine art of paraphrasing and then check your work.

Supreme Court

U.S. Supreme Court Opinions
http://www.law.cornell.edu/supct/index.html

Cornell University offers access to the text and analysis of Supreme Court opinions. You can access the most recent opinions (and dissenting opinions), as well as selected historic decisions. There is also biographical information on each of the Supreme Court justices.

Travel

CDC Home Travel Information Page
http://www.cdc.gov/travel/travel.html

The Center for Disease Control (CDC) posts international travel information. A summary of health information for international travel, called "The Blue Sheet," lists cholera, yellow fever, and plague-infected countries. Information related to immunizations and other preparations for travel-related health conditions is included along with general health recommendations by geographic region.

CityNet
http://www.city.net/

This page is aimed at the traveler and offers information on 2,333 U.S. and international cities. It lists links to the most popular U.S. and international cities.

Country and City Travel Guides
http://www.cclims.com/mall/travel/country.html

This travel guide provides links to countries, cities, states, and regions that have posted information about a city in the United States or abroad. There is a variety of information listed for each area: for example, under South Africa there is information about obtaining a visa, information about an Emergency Travel Clinic, and a national weather forecast for the area.

Country Destinations by Text Express
http://www.lonelyplanet.com/dest/text.htm#count

Designed for tourists, this site gives travel-related and background information on the countries of the world. It includes "Off the Beaten Path" and "Comments by Travelers" links. Travelers' comments are of anthropological interest as they reflect the things tourists find important about their travel experiences. Most comments focus on hotels and cuisine and indicate little interest in the lives and well-being of local peoples.

Currency Converter
http://www.tcn.net/~datatel/currency.html

This Web site is a service of Switzerland-based Olsen & Associates, Ltd. Find an exchange rate on any day from 1990 to the present year. Simply type in the number of U.S. dollars you wish to exchange. Specify the currency of exchange and the date for which you what to know the exchange rate. Select "See the exchange rate."

National Geographic Society
http://www.nationalgeographic.com

This site is best viewed with Netscape or Microsoft Internet Explorer. The National Geographic Society was established in 1888 with the goal to increase geographical knowledge. The society issues three monthly magazines: *National Geographic Magazine*, *National Geographic World*, and *National Geographic Traveler*. Abstracts of the articles in each magazine are available. There is an archive section that summarizes the cover stories for the past six issues. A map section provides political maps, facts, figures, and flags of countries from around the world.

Travel Warnings and Consular Information Sheets
http://travel.state.gov/travel_warnings.html

This U.S. Department of State site provides consular information sheets, travel warnings, and public announcements on every country in the world. The travel warnings are State Department recommendations to avoid travel to certain countries. Consular information sheets include factual information of interest to travelers, such as the location of the U.S. embassy or consulate, unusual entry regulations and immigration practices, health conditions, political disturbances, crime and security information, and drug penalties. Public announcements provide information about terrorist threats and other conditions the government believes pose risks to American travelers.

Web of Culture
http://www.worldculture.com/

E. F. Sheridan, president of The Web of Culture and also an
independent consultant, developed this Web site for a graduate course
in cross-cultural communications. This site offers information useful to
those about to travel abroad, as well as to those who are interested in
learning more about customs and practices in other cultures. Some
topics covered include gestures (did you know that the "ok" hand
gesture in America is considered an obscene gesture in Spain?),
currency (including exchange rates), holidays and international
headlines. There is also a language link which allows you to identify
the language(s) you speak and the ones you want to learn. The
computer displays common words and phrases in your native language
and gives a translation in the language you want to learn. If you have
specific questions about a culture, this site includes a "Cultural
Contact" which allows you to pose your questions directly to a "native"
of that culture using e-mail.

Yahoo! Weather
http://weather.yahoo.com/index.html

Select a region of the world and then the country to which you will be
traveling. Selected cities in the chosen countries are listed for which
you can get a five-day weather forecast in Celsius or Fahrenheit,
satellite photos, and a report on atmospheric conditions.

U.S. Government Agencies

Bureau of Indian Affairs
http://www.doi.gov/bureau-indian-affairs.html

The U.S. Department of Interior, Bureau of Indian Affairs, is
"responsible for the administration of federal programs for federally
recognized Indian tribes, and for promoting Indian self-determination."
The link "American Indian Heritage Day" gives access to the full text
of the proclamation by President Clinton declaring the month of
November "National American Indian Heritage Month." There are
links to other documents chronicling the effort to set aside special days,
weeks, and months of the year to honor Native Americans. There is
also information on the meaning of Indian ancestry and information on
how to do genealogical research. The BIA press releases cover court
decisions that affect Native American communities.

Central Intelligence Agency
http://www.odci.gov/cia/ciahome.html

Since 1947 the Central Intelligence Agency has been in the business of collecting and conducting information on developments in foreign countries. For an overview of the CIA and its operations, take the "virtual tour" of Central Intelligence Agency. The 1996 *World Factbook* contains a wide range of information on all countries and bodies of water and is available at this Web site. The 1995 *Factbook on Intelligence* can also be accessed. CIA Press Releases and Statements often contain useful information of interest to anthropologists as reflected in the following headlines: "The Outlook for China: A CIA Perspective," "CIA Executive Director Statement on Persian Gulf Veteran Illness," and "CIA Shares Technology with the Navajo Nation."

National Institutes of Health
http://www.nih.gov/

The National Institutes of Health (NIH) mission is "to uncover new knowledge that will lead to better health for everyone." As of March 24, 1997, the NIH database contains 49,085 documents on 159 NIH Internet services. In light of the large number of documents perhaps the best way to approach this Web site is to use its search engine. Keywords relevant to those interested in medical anthropology include: - alternative medicine, holistic medicine, culture, women's health, immigration, and special populations (Native Americans, Latin Americans, etc.).

U.S. Department of Health and Human Services
http://www.os.dhhs.gov/

The Department of Health and Human Services (DHHS) is a government agency charged with the tasks of protecting the health of all Americans and of providing basic services, especially to the most disadvantaged segments of the population. The DHHS encompasses more than 300 programs engaged in a wide range of activities (e.g., preventing outbreaks of infectious diseases, immunization, assisting low-income families, preventing child abuse). The News and Public Affairs link gives access to the news, speeches and press releases since 1991. Titles include "Disability Rate Among Older Americans Declines Dramatically," "The Tyranny of Thinness Obsession" and "Cancer Research in Brief."

U.S. Department of State Home Page
http://www.state.gov/

The U.S. Department of State Home Page offers information on U.S. foreign policy by region: Africa (sub-Saharan), East Asia and the Pacific, Europe and Canada, the Americas (Latin America and the Caribbean), the Middle East and North Africa, the New Independent States of the Former USSR, and South Asia. There is also information about U.S. foreign policy as it relates to global issues such as population, refugees, human rights, and arms control. The *Country Background Notes* are general sources of information about people, government, political conditions, economy, history, defense, foreign relations, and travel for countries in Africa, Middle East and North Africa, East Asia and the Pacific, South Asia, Europe, Canada, Latin America and the Caribbean. The "Hot Topics" link highlights foreign policy issues in the news.

U.S. Federal Government Agencies
http://www.lib.lsu.edu/gov/fedgov.html

The Louisiana State University Library System posts a list of links to more than 100 U.S. federal government agencies and departments. The following agencies are of particular interest to anthropologists: Department of Energy, Administration on Aging, Indian Health Service, Department of Health and Human Services, Bureau of Indian Affairs, and Bureau of Land Management.

U.S. National Library of Medicine
http://www.nlm.nih.gov/nlmhome.html

The National Library of Medicine (NLM) "provides a wide variety of resources related to biomedical and health science, both past and present." Some particularly interesting features include:
1) The newsletter *AIDS Treatment News*, beginning with the April 8, 1988 issue.
2) Online exhibitions of art, history, and images connected with medicine.
3) Images from the history of medicine including nearly 60,000 prints, photographs, and artwork from the history of medicine division.
4) Visible human images link connects you to a sample of anatomic images of male and female humans.

United States Information Agency
http://www.usia.gov/

The mission of the United State Information Agency (USIA) is "to understand, inform, and influence foreign publics in promotion of the national interest, and to broaden the dialogue between Americans and U.S. institutions and their counterparts abroad." This agency coordinates with other countries in the world to promote education and cultural exchanges. At this site, there are links to U.S. institutions and their counterparts overseas, the Fulbright Exchange Program (which operates in 125 countries), citizen and professional exchange programs, Foreign Students Advising (which gives information and advice to those interested in studying in the United States), and youth exchange programs. There is also a link to the *Daily Digest* of foreign media commentary and reaction to major U.S. foreign policy issues or events. The latest reports and archived issues can be accessed.

Weather

Yahoo! Weather
http://weather.yahoo.com/index.html

Select a region of the world and then the country to which you will be traveling. Selected cities in the chosen countries are listed for which you can get a five-day weather forecast in Celsius or Fahrenheit, satellite photos, and a report on atmospheric conditions.

World Leaders

Heads of State and Heads of Government
http://www.geocities.com/Athens/1058/rulers.html

This site lists all heads of state and other top-ranking leaders (past and present) of all currently existing countries and territories, including term of office and year of birth and death (if applicable). It lists leaders (past and present) of the Arab League, European Union, Organization of African Unity, the Organization of American States, and the United Nations. A special section chronicles the changes in leadership since January 1996.

Social, Humanitarian, and Culture Committee
http://www.umich.edu/~michmun/Links/sochum.html

University of Michigan Model United Nations (UMMUN) is a conference that draws high school students from around the country in which they assume roles of UN delegates from foreign countries. This Web page contains three reports from the Social, Humanitarian, and Culture Committee on topics including female genital mutilation, population planning, and AIDS in Africa.

Zipcode-Level Information

U.S. Gazetteer
http://www.census.gov/cgi-bin/gazetteer

This Census Bureau site allows users to submit a zip code and/or the name of a city in the United States to get the population and location in terms of latitude (position north or south of the equator measured from 0° to 90°) and longitude (position to the east or west of an imaginary line running north and south around the world). Select "STF1A" or "STF3a" to choose among approximately 100 tables giving information on subjects ranging from age composition to the number of vacant housing units. If you have Netscape or another graphical browser, select "Map" to view a map of the city or zip code area.

United States Postal Service Zip Code Lookup and Address Information
http://www.usps.gov/ncsc/

Submit a city name and its zip code appears. Submit a zip code and the name of the city to which that zip code has been assigned appears. The U.S. Postal Service answers commonly asked questions about zip codes and makes recommendations for addressing mail.

Part III

College Experience

Campus Newspapers

Campus Newspapers on the Internet
http://beacon-www.asa.utk.edu/resources/papers.html

This site is posted by *The Daily Beacon*, the student newspaper at the University of Tennessee, Knoxville. In addition there are links to hundreds of other college newspapers. Depending on the site, you can access the current issue, recent issues, and/or archived issues.

Colleges and Universities

Academe This Week
http://chronicle.merit.edu/.almanac/.almanac.html

This is a statistical portrait of higher education in the United States. It includes statistics on graduation rates at NCAA Division I institutions, the number of college degrees awarded, the average pay of full-time professors, and enrollment by age, sex, and race.

COLLEGEXPRESS
http://www.collegexpress.com/index.html

Interested in finding out information on a college or university in the United States? CollegeExpress allows you to find out about tuition costs, location, characteristics of student populations, and so on. Once you have registered, select colleges that you would like to know more about and receive information from them. If you are interested in graduate school, check out the graduate school link which posts advice about how to (1) select a graduate program (2) improve chances of being accepted, and (3) prepare for tests. There is also information about financial aid/scholarships, including information on how school officials judge applications and the different types of financial aid. This site is best viewed using Netscape.

FastWEB
http://www.studentservices.com/fastweb/

Looking for money to pay for school? FastWEB (Financial Aid Search through the WEB) offers over 180,000 listings of scholarships, fellowships, grants, and loans. Simply complete the application to set up your FastWEB mailbox. Based on the information in your application, FastWEB provides you with a list of awards for which you may be eligible, including information about the dollar amount of the award, addresses to send inquiries, and deadlines for applications. FastWEB sends you updated information on any new funding opportunities that have been posted after your initial registration.

List of American Universities Home Pages
http://www.clas.ufl.edu/CLAS/american-universities.html

This site gives the home pages of American universities granting bachelor or advanced degrees. It provides links to international universities, Canadian universities, and community colleges as well.

Preparing Your Student for College
http://www.ed.gov/pubs/Prepare/

This U.S. Department of Education guidebook covers areas such as choosing a college, financing an education, and doing long-range planning. The guidebook also lists and defines important terms related to the college experience, such as B.A. and B.S.

Financial Aid

FastWEB
http://www.studentservices.com/fastweb/

Looking for money to pay for school? FastWEB (Financial Aid Search through the WEB) offers over 180,000 listings of scholarships, fellowships, grants, and loans. Simply complete the application to set up your FastWEB mailbox. Based on the information in your application, FastWEB provides you with a list of awards for which you may be eligible, including information about the dollar amount of the award, addresses to send inquiries, and deadlines for applications. FastWEB sends you updated information on any new funding opportunities that have been posted after your initial registration.

Funding College
http://www.ed.gov/prog_info/SFA/FYE/index.html

This U.S. Department of Education publication provides information about federal financial aid programs for college students.

Preparing Grant and Scholarship Applications
http://edziza.arts.ubc.ca/arts/anso/funding.htm#grant

This site, produced and maintained by the University of British Columbia Anthropology Department, offers graduate students some advice for preparing grant and scholarship applications. Some suggestions include defining your goals for research, making sure your research is feasible, and outlining procedures to be used in your research.

Scholarships and Fellowships
http://web.studentservices.com/search/

Searching for money to fund education is as easy as entering your name, address, and major. A list of scholarships for which you might be eligible will appear on the screen, and information about other scholarships for which you might be eligible will be e-mailed to you as they become available.

Graduate School

1995 Survey of Anthropology Ph.D.s
http://www.ameranthassn.org/95survey.htm

The American Anthropological Association surveys new Ph.D. recipients of anthropology every two years. The AAA has posted the 1995 results of a survey of 300, 1994-1995 new anthropology Ph.D.s. The report posts findings related to the demographic profiles of the typical anthropology Ph.D. (sex, age, race/ethnicity), areas of specialization, time taken to complete the Ph.D., job prospects, and salaries. There is also invaluable advice from the new Ph.Ds about how to make the best of the graduate school experience and their answers to the question, "Would they do it all again?"

Graduate School Guide
http://www.schoolguides.com/

This guide to graduate schools in the eastern and southern regions of the country allows users to search by field of study or state. E-mail addresses are given for those schools with graduate programs, as well as addresses and phone numbers.

Guide to Graduate School
http://www.jobtrak.com/gradschool_docs/gradschool

The UCLA Placement and Career Planning Center posts this site, which answers FAQ's about graduate school. The menu includes the following topics: "Graduate School" (the basics), "Making the Decision," "Selecting a School," "Criteria for Evaluating a Graduate Program," "The Application Process" (which includes a personal essay and faculty recommendations), "Financing Graduate Studies," "Graduate School Tests," and "Reference/Resource Material."

Graduate Student Resources on the Web
http://www-personal.umich.edu/%7Edanhorn/graduate.html

This University of Michigan Web site posted by Dan Horn, a graduate student in the Department of Psychology's Cognition and Perception Program, is a list of links to various sites that provide information related to every aspect of graduate school from the application process to the dissertation. Also be sure to check out the "humor" link as it includes some interesting advice in a light format. For example, be sure to check out "How to Receive a Less than Enthusiastic Letter of Recommendation."

Study Skills

ERIC Digests
http://www.ed.gov/databases/ERIC.Digests/

ERIC is a clearinghouse for educational material. The following are selected ERIC publications related to study skills and the college experience. Use the numbers to the left of the titles listed below followed by .html to complete the URL address above (e.g. http://www.ed.gov/databases/ERIC_Digests/**ed325659.html**)

250694 Qualities of Effective Writing Programs
250696 Vocabulary
291205 Critical Presentation Skills—Research to Practice
296347 Audience Awareness: When and How Does It Develop?
300805 Note-Taking: What Do We Know About the Benefits?
301143 Learning Styles
302558 Improving Your Test-Taking Skills

Textbooks

Student Market
http://www.studentmkt.com/

Tired of waiting in long lines at the bookstore to pay high prices for used books, or having to post flyers around school to sell your books? This site has a solution. Student market allows students to post textbooks for sale on their Web site and to search for textbooks to purchase. It also allows you to search specific colleges for textbooks for sale. Best viewed using Netscape 2.0 or higher or Internet Explorer 3.0 or higher.

Part IV

Career Opportunities

America's Job Bank
http://www.ajb.dni.us/

This site is a combined effort of the U.S. Department of Labor and 1,800 state public employment service agencies located throughout the United States. Approximately 250,000 job listings in areas throughout the United States and its territories are linked through America's Job Bank, making this site the largest compilation of active job opportunities available anywhere. This site gives links to private career placement agencies located throughout the United States.

Careers in Archaeology
http://www.museum.state.il.us/ismdepts/anthro/dlcfaq.html

This site, maintained by Texas A&M University, gives answers to some of the most frequently asked questions about to careers in archaeology. The questions range from (1) What jobs are available for archaeologists? (2) What education and training are required to become a professional archaeologist? (3) What college or university should I go to? (4) What are some general introductory books on archaeology? (5) I want to go on a dig. How do I volunteer? (6) Where can I get more information on archaeology?

Careers in Archaeology in the U.S. (FAQ)
http://www.museum.state.il.us/ismdepts/anthro/dlcfaq.html

Prof. David L. Carlson of Texas A&M University identifies and answers frequently asked questions about a career in archaeology. Questions are related to jobs, education, and training. Carlson also recommends general/introductory sources on archaeology fieldwork (digs).

Career Development Manual
http://www.adm.uwaterloo.ca/infocecs/CRC/manual-home.html

The University of Waterloo posts the Career Development Manual, which covers the "Steps to the Right Job": (1) self-assessment (2) researching occupations (3) decision making about long- and short-term occupational goals (4) taking the steps to find employment, and (5) evaluating job offers and accepting the job.

Career Magazine
http://www.careermag.com

This site provides access to over 14,000 current job listings from around the world. It also has information such as salary resources, information on companies that recruit college graduates, and informative news articles.

CareerPath
http://www.careerpath. com/

From this site it's possible to search newspaper employment ads from 10 major cities. There is no fee charged for this service, but you must register to use it.

Career Shop's Resume, Job and Employment Site
http://www.careershop.com/

This site is "an online database of resume profiles and employment opportunities, designed to assist job seekers and hiring employers alike. Job seekers can post resume profiles in your resume database and perform job searches of your Job Openings database—online and free of charge!" There is also advice on preparing for an interview and promoting yourself to employers.

ERIC Digests
http://www.ed.gov/databases/ERIC_DIGESTS

ERIC is a clearinghouse for educational material. The following are ERIC publications related to jobs/careers. Use the numbers to the left of the titles listed below followed by .html to complete the URL above (e.g. http://www.ed.gov/databases/ERIC_Digests/**ed325659.html**)

292974 Workplace Literacy Programs
346318 Job Search Methods
376274 Job Search Skills for the Current Economy

Major Resource Kit
http://www.udel.edu/CSC/choosing.html

The University of Delaware has compiled a "Major Resource Kit" for 49 undergraduate programs to help new graduates in their search for a job. Each kit includes information such as the job titles recent graduates have attained that directly relate to their major. This site tells the amount of education required for specific jobs, and it also gives tips for increasing employability. A few words of warning: the kinds of jobs listed may *not* be representative of the jobs for which a major may be eligible to apply. For example, the jobs listed for anthropology clearly understate the wide range of occupations anthropologists hold.

Occupational Outlook Handbook
http://stats.bls.gov/ocohome.htm

The Bureau of Labor Statistics publishes this career guidance handbook, which lists comprehensive job descriptions, including their educational and other qualifications, working conditions, earnings, employment trends, and job prospects. Users of *The Occupational Outlook Handbook* can browse by job title or search by keyword, such as "social scientist." The handbook is revised every two years.

Resume-O-Matic
http://www.ypn.com/jobs/resumes/index.html

Resume-O-Matic makes it easy to post your resume on the Internet. Simply answer the questions, and Resume-O-Matic will turn your answers into a resume that will be posted on the Web for a full year free of charge.

Career Choices in Anthropology

When Michael Crichton, author of *Jurassic Park*, was asked by *Time Magazine* the inevitable question about how his career as a best-selling writer developed, Crichton answered that he "went to Harvard in 1960 intending to be a writer. But the English department rubbed a blister on his soul (it was 'not the place for an aspiring writer,' he said; 'it was the place for an aspiring English professor'), so he switched to anthropology."

In fact, there are several successful literary types who began their careers with a solid foundation in anthropology. The famous science fiction authors Kurt Vonnegut, Jr., Ursula K. Le Guin, and Chad Oliver are examples. Steve Riggio, the founder of the Barnes and Noble mega-bookstore chain, was an anthropology major. In the arts, singers Tracy Chapman and Mick Jagger were also drawn to anthropology. In the realm of politics, anthropology majors include the first president of Kenya, Jomo Kenyatta, and the current Congressman from Ohio's second district, Rob Portman. There are even examples of royalty in the persons of Prince Charles of England and Prince Peter of Greece and Denmark. Jane Goodall is an anthropologist. And the list goes on.

Interest in and respect for anthropology are growing, and in 1995 (the most recent year for which we have statistics) more anthropology degrees were awarded in the United States than in any other single year. The number of anthropology students continues to rise. According to the American Anthropological Association, in the last ten years the number of anthropology majors has increased 109%.

National Public Radio reports that the World Bank is restructuring and plans to hire fewer economists and more anthropologists. Anthropologists, it is felt, will best be able to understand the financial needs of businesses in other countries. It is assumed that anthropologists will make the projects of the World Bank more relevant and more cost-effective.

We all know that a college degree—in just about anything—increases one's lifetime earnings and decreases the chances of unemployment. (According to the Bureau of Labor Statistics, the difference in the earnings gap between college and high school graduates is 60% and growing; a *New York Times* study of job losses shows that it is high school graduates who account for 66% of all people who have lost their jobs.)

So college is a good idea, but is anthropology the career path you should take in college? If so, what areas of anthropology offer the most promise? Before getting down to the basics of where the jobs are, I would like to address what, in my opinion, is an even more important issue: what would you enjoy doing for the next forty or fifty years of your life?

While the least a career should do is offer you a salary and some security, I think it should offer much more. Therefore, I ask you to consider this advice: Before you ask the questions of where are the most jobs and how much money you can make, I suggest you ask yourself what you enjoy.

I *love* being an anthropologist. At times it offers all the excitement of an *Indiana Jones* story and all the challenge of a Tony Hillerman mystery. I will never forget riding horses in Canyon de Chelly with a Navajo guide in search of Anasazi ruins or living in a remote, haunted cabin on the Cherokee reservation. I have danced around a campfire, my face painted with magical designs, and I have slept under the stars. I have climbed inside the Great Pyramid in Egypt and stood atop the Pyramid of the Moon in Mexico. As an applied cultural anthropologist, I have researched and written a report that stopped a highway from barreling through an Indian reservation. And every time I do something like that, I marvel that I actually get paid to be an anthropologist.

If I won the lottery tomorrow and never had to work another day in my life, I would not quit my job because the money is only one of the reasons I am an anthropologist. I suggest you ask yourself the question of what gives you so much pleasure that even if you won the lottery, you would not quit. I think that question should be the first that you ask yourself in your quest for a career.

But you should also know that I enjoy the more contemplative tasks that go into being an anthropologist, too, at least as I define anthropology. I enjoy teaching, even topics like kinship terminology, and watching the faces of my students as they "get it" for the first time. I enjoy analyzing my research and the thrill that comes when I "get it" for the first time. I enjoy writing books and articles about the people I have studied and realizing that long after I am dead someone will pull from a library shelf—or punch up on the Internet—a book I have written and feel some of the same wonder I did so long ago.

How do *you* define anthropology? What would give *you* pleasure? How will *you* make a living out of something that gives you satisfaction? Some areas of anthropology are more popular than others. Most of us, often as children, have read the story of archaeologist Howard Carter as he gazed upon the treasures of King Tut's tomb for the first time. Archaeology is a subfield of anthropology. Forensic anthropology is another popular subfield, and I realized recently just how popular when I ran across a children's book, *The Bone Detectives: How Forensic Anthropologists Solve Crimes and Uncover Mysteries of the Dead*. Archaeology and forensic anthropology both seem like such interesting ways of making a living. Is that possible? The answer is yes and no.

For archaeology, the answer is a loud yes. There are dozens and dozens of contract archaeology companies operating in the United States and hiring people at every college degree level from the bachelor's degree to the doctorate. Throw in universities and museums that hire archaeologists, and the job market is even bigger. And that is true of archaeology all over the world. So, if your interest is archaeology, go to it.

What about forensic anthropology? Exciting? Yes. Jobs that pay money? Only for the lucky few. There are only about 150 forensic anthropologists in the United States, and only about 15 of them work full-time as forensic anthropologists. The rest of them do forensic anthropology part-time and support themselves working in related areas of anthropology, biology, or medicine. Part-timers might get only one or two grizzly cases a year. If your interest is forensic anthropology, you need to decide how the availability of work affects your career choice. Could you be happy earning your living in a related area of anthropology where there are numerous jobs and do forensics here and there?

Other job prospects in anthropology lie somewhere along the continuum between archaeology and forensic anthropology. Applied anthropology and environmental studies lie closer to archaeology along the job continuum. College teaching has slipped toward the forensic anthropology end of the continuum when it comes to new jobs as a professor (although that seems to be changing for the better). Could you be happy teaching in college part-time and making your living as a contract archaeologist or an applied researcher?

As may be obvious by now, my mission is not only to give you the answers in your career search, but also to help you pose the questions important to you. What should your strategy be in your quest for a career in anthropology? That is something for you to decide. But I can tell you what I would do, with what I know now, if I were just starting out.

I would have a two-pronged approach. I would prepare myself to go after the career in anthropology I most wanted, job availability or not. But then, when it comes to career, I am willing to be a risk taker. But even risk takers hedge their bets. The second part of my approach would be to amass as many job skills as possible in every area of anthropology and related fields, especially those areas where jobs are more readily available. The most important question you can answer for yourself is what your approach should be.

Follow your heart, but in a pragmatic sort of way. Take courses that will develop important skills: anthropology courses such as ethnographic methods, museum methods, laboratory methods, and archaeology field school and courses outside of anthropology such as statistics, a foreign language, computer skills, historical research, photography, and sociological methods. Accumulate work experience, even if at first you have to do it on a volunteer basis, with museums, contract archaeology companies, and human services organizations.

Continue your career research by talking with anthropology faculty and alumni. Browse the American Anthropological Association's *Guide to Departments of Anthropology*. Surf the AAA's Web site (at http://www.ameranthassn.org) and other careers sites listed here in *Let's Go Anthropology*. Consider whether graduate school is something you do or do not want to attend. Read books and articles on the various subfields. Take more anthropology courses.

I wish you all the best in your career quest.

by Sharlotte Neely, Ph.D.,
Professor and Coordinator,
Northern Kentucky University
Anthropology Program
Email: Neelys@nku.edu